MANIPULATIVE TECHNIQUES

Detecting manipulation, repulsing it and using it in a targeted manner

by Alexander Hellmoldt

Table of Contents

1. Preface

"It is very easy to mislead men by means of great and clumsy representations; but if the reasonable and the decent are presented to them in an interesting way, they will certainly grasp it."

Johann Wolfgang von Goethe (1749 - 1832)

Why do some people manage again and again to bring others to something that they don't really want? Why do we accept arguments and points of view, even though we realize internally that we are acting against our own will and interests? The answer to these questions is quite simple: we are manipulated.

Every person is manipulated daily, hourly, even minutely - sometimes without realizing it. You don't believe that? It gets even better: You manipulate day after day, hour after hour. Why? Because every human being, consciously or unconsciously is programmed for his own advantage, for the satisfaction of his own needs and for his own satisfaction. We humans simply cannot manipulate. With a little practice and training, however, we can prevent ourselves from being manipulated. How this works is explained in this book.

2. What we understand by manipulation

*Andrea Mira Meneghin (*1967)*

Manipulation can happen at any time and in any place where we deal with other people: in professional negotiations, in discussions, in criticism and conflict talks, and even in conversations with friends and our partner. In order to be able to defend oneself against manipulations, it is important to recognize them first, no matter in which form they occur.

Manipulation is the conscious or unconscious use of different behaviours, which influence the behavior or decisions of another person.

Manipulation can be divided into:

- **active manipulation:** we manipulate another human being,

- **passive manipulation**: we are manipulated by another person or media,

and:

- **conscious manipulation:** we notice it when we ourselves are manipulated or when we manipulate other people,

- **unconscious manipulation**: we do not notice that we manipulate other people, or are manipulated by them or by the media.

The best example of passive manipulation is advertising. For example, companies use advertising on television, the Internet or in newspapers to influence our purchasing decisions and to get us enthusiastic about a particular product or service. This is a form of conscious manipulation in which our purchasing decisions are to be influenced.

However, manipulation does not always require a clever strategy; it can also happen unconsciously. We use this tactic again and again to get our wishes or needs fulfilled.

Example: Your partner asks you for a favor, which you initially refuse. In response, your partner says, "It's okay, I'm used to it." With this supposedly final answer, your partner signals that you have disappointed him many times in the past and left him alone with his needs and desires. His goal is to change your mind, so that you still fulfill what he or she the wished for.

2.1 Why is manipulation unfair?

The aim of any manipulation is to persuade another person to act, think or behave in a certain way. For this reason, manipulation is unfair, because fairness means that every person has a right to protect his own interests and to adopt other points of view only of his own free will and insight. So when I circumcise a person in his right to represent his own interests and put my points of view, which he voluntarily does not want to accept, I am acting unfairly towards that person.

It follows from this approach that a **manipulator wants to achieve a certain goal using unfair means.**

2.2 How can you deal with manipulation?

The problem with manipulations is that in some cases, you don't know exactly what the manipulator is trying to do. In addition, there are countless techniques to manipulate other people. In order to bring some structure into this problem, three steps are necessary:

1) Recognize and repel the manipulation technique

2) Understanding the strategy and intention of the manipulator

3) Implementation of (fair) counter measures

Especially, the first step is important, because you first have to expose the respective manipulation technique in order to be able to carry out fair counter measures. These counter measures have to be learned and practiced first. You will learn them later in this book.

At this point, let us go into the three individual steps in more detail before we turn to the basic rules of how you can deal with manipulation.

Step 1: Recognize and ward off manipulation techniques

You can only protect yourself against manipulation techniques if you can identify them beforehand. In this book, you'll find some simple, yet very effective protection techniques that you can use in various situations. The aim of these protection techniques is to immediately and elegantly prevent the respective manipulation technique.

Step 2: Understanding the intention and strategy of the manipulator

If you feel that you are being manipulated, consider what the manipulator's intention is and what strategy it is using. For this purpose, you will learn a simple classification system that will help you to recognize and understand manipulation situations faster in this guide. The goal is to recognize the intention of the manipulator.

Step 3: Implementation of fair countermeasures

Once you have recognized the intention of the manipulator, you can react accordingly. For this, you will learn effective and simple procedures, which you can use in numerous situations. The aim of this counter-strategy is to protect your own interests in a fairly.

2.3 Important basic rules for handling manipulations

There are important basic rules which you should know and heed when dealing with manipulations.

Basic Rule 1: Stay fair and objective
Surely, this is the golden rule when it comes to dealing with other people. Make sure that both your argumentation and that of your interlocutor remain objective, and that comprehensible reasons are the basis for your exchange.

Basic Rule 2: Always stay cool
A discussion can sometimes be heated, because every person is different and has different views of which he himself is firmly convinced. He may not understand that you do not want to share his views and opinions. But also stay calm in such tricky situations. A few basic methods will help you with this, which you will learn in this book.

Basic rule 3: Don't forget your rights!
Everyone has untouchable rights - including you! You don't always have to say "Yes and Amen" to everything. It is perfectly ok, and your absolute right to defend yourself against manipulative attacks.

So don't forget that you have the right:

- ✓ To say no without feeling guilty.

- ✓ To be treated with respect by your fellow human beings.

- ✓ To express your feelings, wishes and opinions.

- ✓ To be allowed to set priorities.

- ✓ To be allowed to represent your own point of view, even if it may not be in conformity with that of other people.

- ✓ To protect you from emotional, moral and physical attacks.

- ✓ AND BEFORE EVERYTHING, to live your life **according to your own ideas**.

When you meet manipulative characters, it is very important to remember these principles again and again. Why? Manipulative people do not respect the boundaries of other people, and always push them to their limits.

Basic rule 4: Acting and not reacting causally

If we are manipulated, we usually reveal typical defensive reactions. We perceive the behaviour of the manipulator as emotional or unfair, and as a result, we also react with emotionality and unfair answers. In some cases, however, we give in or escape communication.

In this way, however, we give the manipulator exactly what he/she actually wanted to achieve unconsciously or consciously. He/she speculated exactly on these reactions from us.

A successful manipulation basically involves a certain stimulus-response mechanism. If we want to keep conversation control, we have to break through this mechanism.

Basic rule 5: Don't lose sight of the goal

Talking to a manipulative person can be exhausting. It is therefore more important that you do not allow yourself to take the initiative in the conversation, but persistently and stubbornly pursue your discussion goals. Do not let the manipulator distract you from your goal. It is helpful to define a certain goal before the conversation, which you can always keep in mind during the conversation.

Basic rule 6: Put your focus on concrete behaviours

Do not make the mistake and interpret the behaviour you observe as the behaviour of a particular type of person. If you think "He is a wimp" or "She is a very difficult person", you filter and order all your perceptions with the help of these typifications, and thus inevitably run into a trap. Why? This way, you miss the opportunity to turn the conversation around positively. Instead, pay more attention to concrete behaviours, and if something disturbs you about the behavior of your counterpart, then talk about it quite openly.

Basic rule 7: Building golden bridges

An important goal in conversations with manipulative people should be to give communication a solution-oriented and objective character again. You should therefore offer your interlocutor such an opportunity, even if he/she has behaved off-key. In this way, a re-entry into the cooperation is possible.

3. Common manipulation techniques

"Manipulation: Tutoring for the Just Course of Things."

*Andreas Egert (*1968), German journalist,*
publicist and aphorist.

I have compiled a selection of manipulation techniques, which I will discuss in more or less detail below. With these methods, you can both manipulate people and better understand whether you are being manipulated yourself.

Some of the techniques are similar and many build on each other. They can be used whenever it is appropriate. However, manipulation techniques do not replace the homework that you have to do as a salesman, for example. Those who do not know their products, do not know how to calculate a price, or do not dress properly will not achieve much even with the best technology.

Moreover, manipulation techniques are not secret knowledge. Just as you learn to manipulate other people here, you learn at the same time how to defend yourself - by being aware of these techniques. So if your counterpart is also familiar with manipulation, it may well be that you have to adapt your strategies.

Basically, one can distinguish between two different approaches: Addressing instincts and gaining dominance. With instincts, we address ancient behaviours that are anchored in us, and that we can hardly consciously avoid. In dominance, we try to be superior to the opponent.

3.1 Manipulation with the Dominance Approach

With this approach, you are trying to gain control over your counterpart, so to speak. The aim of all methods is to be faster than the other, and to take him by surprise with your dominance. Often, this happens so subtly that the manipulated person doesn't even notice. In contrast to instincts, here, behavior patterns are exploited which are acquired by us and which actually have a positive effect, such as trusting sympathetic people. But this can also be exploited. While instinct manipulation actually works for everyone, you should be able to assess your opponent well with the dominance methods in order to select the appropriate tactic.

3.1.1 Block

Another manipulation technique is blocking the conversation partner. This is expressed for example by the fact that your counterpart does not give an answer to a question of yours, or more or less cleverly avoids the core of the question again and again.

It is also part of the manipulation technique of blocking if your interlocutor either does not want to understand you, or deliberately misunderstands you. He may also turn the proverbial word in your mouth.

What does this do to you? The first time, you will certainly try to formulate your question differently, so that your interlocutor understands the core of your question. At the second or third time, you will probably withdraw the question unnerved and will refrain from an answer. When this happens, the manipulator has reached his/her goal, which is to avoid the question that is uncomfortable for them. Many politicians, by the way, understand this form of manipulation very well.

Everyday/practical example

You denied your partner a wish. He then ignores your further questions and treats you as if you were literally air. He tries to elude communication with you. What is his purpose?

With his behavior he might want to make you refuse any wishes from him in the future and he shows you with his current behavior, whose consequences threaten you otherwise. He may also try to change your mind for his rejected wish and uses this manipulation technique for this purpose.

This manipulative behavior is particularly common because, every human being strives from birth to be noticed.

3.1.2 Enforcement

Generate time pressure, build up emotions or even lie, threaten and personally attack the conversation partner. All these are particularly "dirty" possibilities of manipulation, which fall into the area of "enforcement". In this case, the manipulation is not subtle or elegant, but is done with the "wooden hammer method", especially with the instruments lies, threats and personal attack. This also includes creating artificial time pressure on the other person.

Everyday/practical examples:

<u>**Case 1:**</u>

"This offer is only valid today!"

"If you order within the next ten minutes, you'll get three more products for free."

"If you order by 5pm, the product will be shipped to you today."

"Only 15 minutes left until this unique offer expires!"

Do these sentences look familiar to you? Certainly, because nowadays, advertising relies exactly on this form of manipulation technique. They know that we humans hate to have the feeling to miss a good offer. The aim of this form of manipulation is to motivate you to make a quick -

and less deliberate purchase decision. You should not think long about the practical use or your financial possibilities, but follow your buying and hunting instinct. With these offers, you lack the possibility to check whether the respective offers are actually limited in time - but with this form of manipulation technique, this is ultimately also indifferent, because the seller simply wants to achieve a quick deal by creating a feeling of pressure within you. However, hurrying is rarely a good advise, and for this reason you will perhaps be annoyed a little later that you have been put under time pressure with your purchase decision. You might not have chosen this product or service if you had had more time to think before you bought it.

<u>Case **2:**</u>

"If you don't clean your room, I don't love you anymore!"

If-then-statements *are almost always forms of manipulation that are supposed to get you to do a certain thing. This example may seem familiar to you from your childhood, and is a particularly blatant form of manipulation. With this threat, your interlocutor tries to manipulate you to do his will. Your father or mother could no longer see how messy your room was. For this reason, they took this form of manipulation and wanted to motivate you to get your room in order by threatening to withdraw their love. The form of threatening manipulation* *therefore works with fears that are stirred up in you - in this case, the fear of no longer being loved.*

<u>Case **3:**</u>

"If you don't want to choose this product today, I can't guarantee I'll have it in stock tomorrow."

This sentence contains two different forms of manipulation from the field of assertiveness. On the one hand, the salesman threatens you with his if-then formulation and on the other hand, he creates time pressure for you. He is betting that you don't want to miss his advertised offer. At the same time, he threatens you with the fact that you could go out empty-handed if you do not decide to buy his product or service now or today.

3.1.3 Sabotage conversations

With this manipulation technique, the manipulator literally bursts the conversation. However, this termination is not necessarily surprising for the manipulator, or happens as an affect - he may have already planned it a few moments or minutes earlier. What is striking about this manipulation technique is that the manipulator does not take responsibility for the abortion of the conversation, but wants to blame the other person for the abortion of the conversation.

Everyday/practical examples:

Case1:

You're talking to your partner or a friend. You get into a heated discussion in your conversation. Maybe it's just a trivial topic, for example who's about to dispose of the garbage can. You make your partner understand that it's his turn. Suddenly, your partner bursts into tears.

How do you feel in this situation? Surely you will have a guilty conscience because you think that you have offended or overtaxed your partner. This emotional outburst can, however, also be played with the aim of creating a bad conscience in you, and getting you to give in and take over the task of "garbage disposal". This form of manipulation ("pressure on the lacrimal gland") is used especially by women with great pleasure and success.

<u>**Case 2:**</u>

Also in this example, you are currently in a discussion with your conversation partner. You cannot understand his argumentation, and ask that he/she explains their point of view to you again more exactly. However, the manipulator refuses to do this. He continues to insist on his point of view without giving you the desired explanation. Further, questions on your part are not answered by him. But he repeats his own view of things again and again.

In this situation, the manipulator already notices that his basis for discussion has been shaken, and that his arguments are running out. But his goal is to convince you of his opinion and his points of view. He tries to enforce this by making you understand that he has already argued sufficiently, and that it is therefore your mistake not to be able or willing to understand him.
In you now, you get the feeling that your interlocutor has actually already put forward enough arguments to prove his point of view or his opinion, and you lack attention or intellect to understand this.

In both cases, the manipulator ends the communication in a one-sided way. He hardly leaves you a possibility to discuss further on a factual level, and to present your arguments to him. In the end, the manipulator wants to create a bad conscience in you, and thus make you adopt his point of view or his opinion.

3.1.4 (lazy) Finding compromises

An extremely popular form of manipulation is to show the counterpart several possible solutions, and to give him a choice between them. The art of the manipulator then lies in offering the desired behavior as a compromise proposal. How does this happen?

The manipulator will offer his counterpart - in addition to the desired behavior - much more extreme suggestions than alternatives. His train of thought behind it: He is very sure that his counterpart will certainly not accept these extreme suggestions. Subsequently, he will be satisfied with the desired suggestion of the questioner, which is significantly more moderate than the other alternatives.

Everyday/practical examples:

<u>Case 1:</u>

You are currently in salary negotiations with your future employer. He gives you the choice to pay you a monthly amount X for your work, say 3,000 Euro gross. He also offers you a company car. However, your salary expectations differ significantly from this offer; you are not looking for a company car, but would rather earn a higher salary, for example 5,000 or 6,000 euros. Your future boss now gives you the choice of accepting his offer or not getting the job at all.

<u>**Case 2:**</u>

A discussion flared up in the office for lunch. The colleagues are not in agreement of whether they should have lunch in the canteen or outside. One colleague - in this case, the manipulator - offers the following compromise:

"Either we eat lunch in the canteen, where the food often doesn't taste really good, or we alternatively go opposite the Greek, where it has always tasted very good to all of us."

The manipulator would like to get his meal wish accepted, in this case, by bad-mouthing his colleagues' food in the canteen. Although he obviously confronts them with a free decision and choice, he clearly influences them by his derogatory statements about the food in the canteen, so that they will in all probability decide in favour of his wish - a visit to the Greek.

3.1.5 Show choices

People can best decide if they have two options to choose from. However, the questioner's choice is not always objective for the other person. Thus, the manipulator can influence the desired choice by the question already.

Everyday/practical example:

You and your partner have had an exhausting and creative day. However, your partner still has the energy to do something. When asked whether you are still doing something with him tonight, you would have the answer "Yes" or "No". Instead, your partner will ask you if you'd rather have dinner or go to the cinema tonight.

On the second question, you now have a concrete choice. It's no longer about whether you want to do anything with your partner, but only about **WHAT** you two could do. Your partner already assumes with his question that you agree to do something with him in the evening. This will make it much more difficult for you to cancel him for the evening, because you don't want to disappoint him. With the first question, this would perhaps be easier for you, because he asks you whether you still want to do something with him at all.

What is especially tricky about this manipulation technique is that you are shown alternatives between two choices. Thus, it is suggested that you have the decision in your hand. However, you may miss out on the fact that your partner has already given you basic approval for an active evening with him, and has not given you a choice in this respect.

3.1.6 Describing of competences

We humans tend to be impressed by certificates or experiences of other humans and to be influenced in our opinion.

A manipulative speaker first explains his competences in detail. His aim here is to maintain the confidence of his interlocutors in his abilities. His interlocutors should rather get involved to join his suggestions or opinions. He must not, however, be too clumsy here, because by simply listing his competences, he would perhaps leave an imaginary and arrogant impression on his interlocutors. Instead, he will describe his competences as casually as possible, in the best case underpinned by certain situations and experiences from his past.

Everyday/practical example:

You yourself are starting a new job. Your colleague introduces himself to you and lets you know again and again that he already has years of experience in the job. This will certainly give you the impression that your new colleague is a competent employee whose advice and opinions must be correct due to his long experience. With an optimal manipulation, you will not objectively put his competence to the test, but more or less blindly accept the advice and opinions of the experienced colleague - under circumstances also with things, which do not concern the concrete work at all, for example political views or private advice.

If you are particularly well versed in an area, you can not only impress, but also manipulate other people. The point of a sales talk is always that the customer believes what you say and that it influences his purchase decision. Just as we believe authorities, we also accept the knowledge of experts and trust them. It is less about facts and details, but about the competence you radiate. You tell the customer how long you've had experience and that you're the best.

Applicable example:

Your customer would like to buy a new laptop, but is overwhelmed with new models and codes. He has a budget that is quite small, and you want to lure more money out of his pocket. In this case, you explain to him how difficult it is to always be up-to-date (creates confidence) and how much time you have spent watching the market and testing new models. You can also say that you have been selling computers for 10 years and the problem has many buyers. If you also say how many customers have bought a cheap computer and it has problems quickly, your customer will be more inclined to accept your expensive offer.

3.1.7 Authority

If you have a profession that radiates a certain authority, you can use it to manipulate other people. Police officers, for example, use this authority to elicit confessions from suspects. Uniforms in particular convey authority, and you can use them to impress your counterpart, so that they follow your instructions. This applies to nurses, but also to less clear uniforms such as company shirts or suits. But it can also be a very self-confident appearance.

Application Example:

You want to raise money for an animal shelter. In order to get enough donations, you ask the shelter to allow you to make yourself an official uniform. It consists of a shirt, a patch on the arm, a name tag attached to the breast pocket, tidy trousers and good shoes. If you now ring the bell at a front door and speak in a calm tone with a low voice, hardly anyone will be able to refuse a small donation.

3.1.8 Precise (fake) facts

Similarly successful as impressing someone with authority is bombarding your counterpart with facts in order to be perceived as an (illusory) expert. Of course, you have to have the facts ready and some tricks. This includes that you take as odd numbers as possible, i.e. do not speak of 70 percent, but of 73 percent. This gives the impression that you have really researched the numbers. Other facts are also possible and you can, for example, refer to studies, scientists or the media. But remember that the more concrete these facts are, the more you can impress and manipulate others (which doesn't mean that they have to be true). Your counterpart will not have a chance to check the facts in a hurry, and will have to believe them.

Application Example:

You want to sell a new software package to a customer. After you have listed all features, you bring facts. These could be: "In the Benchmark test the software finished with 9.4." Or: "96.3 percent of our customers stated in a survey that they would buy the product again". Or: "The software has just been ranked in the top 10 by the computer magazine XY."

3.1.9 Imagine the consequences

We tend to let ourselves be won over to a certain behaviour if we expect positive consequences from it. We follow the principle of reward and punishment. If we are punished for a certain behavior, we reject it - for example, violations of the law with possible fines or imprisonment. On the other hand, behaviors for which we are rewarded, or at least have the prospect of a reward become entrenched in us.

Everyday/practical example:
Your employer offers you a lucrative promotion. However, the prerequisite for this is that you reject your desired transfer to another location. The promotion you are offered would mean an improvement in your work situation and/or your financial situation.

The aim of your boss in this manipulation attempt: he would like to keep you on site. However, you yourself have requested the transfer for family reasons, and would therefore like to change your place of work. But now, you find yourself in a certain dilemma, because you have to decide between your private interests and professional advancement. With this offer, your boss tries to change your mind, because he appreciates your labour. On the one hand, of course, this is a shoulder to shoulder for you and recognition of your work performance, but on the other hand, your boss brings you into a certain dilemma, because you have to choose between professional and private interests.

3.1.10 Iterations

It is well known that the constant drop wears the stone. We humans are easily manipulated by recurring statements. By the way, this is also the decisive basis for a successful autosuggestion. 80 percent of our thinking takes place in the subconscious. If you say the same things to your mind again and again, you will believe them yourself at some point and accept them as correct.

The manipulation tactic of repetition appears again and again in advertising. No company would shoot a commercial to broadcast it only once - the crowd does. In this case, the advertisement tries to brainwash you by reminding you of certain statements about its products, so that they manifest themselves there.

It is interesting to note, by the way, that the increasing number of repetitions of a statement or assertion actually increases the willingness of a person to accept this assertion as perceivable. The reason for this: Repetitions lead to an **awareness effect**, which in turn causes us to adopt a familiar friendly attitude. This strategy makes us much more susceptible to manipulation.

Everyday/practical example:

You attend the well-attended event of a motivational guru. The motivational guru will come up with a chic presentation in which he repeats certain messages over and over again. If the motivational teacher is halfway clever, you will believe his statements and messages sooner or later, even if you may have had a different opinion at the beginning of the event. The manipulation tactics of the motivational guru's repetitions have thus fully worked out in this case.

This tactic is reinforced by the herd instinct in the chosen example. A certain number of people who are open to manipulation, can also cast a spell over you at some point and sweep you away - think here only once of a football match with roaring fans and a great atmosphere in a sold-out stadium.

3.1.11 Compliments

You should actually compliment them to express your appreciation, but you can also use them for your dark side. Compliments mean telling someone how great he or she looks, how strong, sexy, nice, well dressed he or she is. All that flatters the other is a compliment. Why can you manipulate with it? Because we like to get compliments. They strengthen our self-confidence; they make us feel good. Ultimately, you can use it to lure your counterpart. Those who feel so brushed on the belly will hardly resist the next steps. By the way, this can also go so far that you call your counterpart an expert, which is particularly well received in sales techniques.

Application Example:
You don't feel like cooking at all, even though it's your turn today. To get your partner on the stove, you say

that he or she is a true master chef, and his or her food tastes much better than if you were now warming up a can of lentil soup. The more you praise each other and put them on a pedestal, the better. However, this only works a few times in a relationship, so watch out! It's a bit easier in your job: Who tells his boss how good he or she looks today, how beautiful the shoes are, how great the hairstyle is, will probably be less criticized on this day.

3.1.12 Let us be friends

Honestly, it's much less likely to refuse a wish to a friend than to a stranger, isn't it? Exactly! This circumstance is used by this manipulation tactic. The manipulator tries to build up an artificial relationship of trust with his counterpart by mirroring his interlocutor with regard to **body language, common interests and hobbies**.

Often, it is enough to have chosen the right person to manipulate another person. So it is more likely that men buy a car from a male salesman and women are more likely to be tempted by a woman to buy a perfume. We cannot resist sympathy. So if you are sympathetic to your counterpart, there is a good chance that you can manipulate him.

Application Example:
In a department store, a woman is looking for a new blouse. The shop assistant first compliments the

woman on how beautiful her make-up is, and that she has a great hairstyle. She can even start a little small talk, perhaps about the weather. If the customer has chosen a blouse, the sympathy bonus can be taken advantage of by saying "I think it's great for you". Because the saleswoman was already perceived as sympathetic, the opinion counts more than without this preparation.

Everyday/practical example:
Imagine you get a visit from a salesman. Of course, the agent's goal is to sell you a certain product. The agent is quite clever and uses the "Let's be friends trick". So, he starts the conversation with some small talk and you two get to talk about your hobbies. Coincidentally, the agent seems to have exactly the same interests and hobbies as you do. You are happy that you are meeting a person who seems to share your interests. In addition, he doesn't spare praise for you in the conversation and speaks to you after all. You feel flattered and the sales representative immediately seems very sympathetic to you, so that you buy his product with a good feeling.

What happened in this example?
Through this manipulative behaviour, the representative has managed to create a pleasant discussion situation and an almost friendly basis between the two of you. But in the end, he doesn't care about this friendship; his main concern is that you trust him and develop friendly feelings

for him. He knows that you are much more likely to trust a friend, and that the likelihood of you rejecting his products is much lower in a friendly relationship. From the very beginning, however, the agent's goal was not to establish a friendship with you, but to sell his products. You may notice this after the deal if the alleged new friend does not contact you at all.

Above all, people who are alone and like to make contacts with new people fall into this manipulation trap.

3.1.13 Killer phrases

Killer phrases use manslaughter arguments. For example, killer phrases are used to outlaw certain facts or groups of people.

Everyday/practical examples:

<u>Case 1</u>

An example of a killer phrase is the statement "We've always done it this way".

A certain fact is therefore presented as correct, simply because it has existed for a long time. Something is therefore good only because it is already very old.

Well, just because you've always done something that way doesn't mean it's (still) the right thing to do. There are numerous examples from the business world of companies that did not want to adapt their company policy to the requirements of the current time, and subsequently had to file for bankruptcy. Also with these enterprises in the executive committee, it was surely more often said that one always made it in such a way.

In this case, the statement that one has always done it this way simply brings security, supposed calm in the company and legitimation in the respective matter, to put one's feet up and rest on one's laurels.
This statement blocks progress and makes it difficult, especially for young and motivated employees in a company, to contribute their skills accordingly. Again and again, these motivated employees are manipulated by such a killer phrase to adapt to the shenanigans and phlegm in the company and "keep their feet still".

Case 2:
Another example of a killer phrase is the statement "You won't make it anyway".

What does it do to you if you tell a friend or your partner about your career plans and get the answer "You won't make it anyway"? Surely you feel disappointed and angry by this statement. Now there are two possible reactions from you to this statement:

(1) Maybe it is an incentive for you to "really show it to them" and to set your whole ambition on the achievement of your goal.

(2) But it can also turn exactly in the other direction, and you think your counterpart is probably right and you should not even try your ambitious project.

We humans need to feel that we trust our abilities. Exactly, the opposite happens when using this killer phrase. Now, why does the manipulator use this statement? There are several possible reasons for this. Perhaps he himself is dissatisfied with his life or his professional situation, and is not making as much progress as he might wish. Since HE has no professional success, YOU should not have one either, in order not to stand out from you, because we humans always strive for equality. So your friend or partner doesn't want you to be more successful than him, and to be able to put your value above his, so to speak. This may sound complicated, but it is quite logical if you know that every person strives from the ground up to be respected and appreciated. In today's society, however, this esteem is often achieved through professional or private success. Some people often stand in their own way during this process and therefore prefer to block other people's progress in life rather than take their own lives into their own hands. It is easier for them to keep other people "on a small scale" than to climb the next mountain themselves, or to face the next challenge in their lives.

You can certainly see from these two examples for yourself: Killer phrases should be absolutely taboo in conversations with other people. They are demotivating, hurtful and nip any innovation in the bud.

3.1.14 A classic on sale: The Yes-Street

With this method, the other person is driven imperceptibly like a train on rails, which he can no longer leave until the station is reached. He is asked questions that he can only answer with "yes" until he says "yes" to the decisive question.

Application Example:

A customer wants to buy a camera. You can design the question sheet like this:

1. Are you looking for a top model at a super low price?

2. And do you that the image quality is important and also the resolution?

3. You certainly want to have a new model and not the one from 3 years ago, don't you?

4. So you want a good camera, at the best price, with great resolution and modern features?

5. Then this camera XYZ is the right one. Do you want to pay with card or in cash?

3.1.15 Consistency:

A further development of the Yes Street is the consistency method. Here, too, the object to be manipulated must be guided in such a way that it follows a certain argumentation and does not introduce its own thoughts. Here, too, it is a matter of eliciting early approval from the customer. But you can also use this method in a private conversation or in the office. Even if there is suddenly no agreement, you can adapt the strategy and ask new questions, which in turn lead you to the goal.

Application Example:

You want to have some extra vacation days because you want to visit your sick mother. You don't ask for a permit right away, but you ask if your boss would visit his sick mother, even if she lives further away. Then you report about a friend who got unpaid leave in such a situation and ask your boss what he thinks about this decision. Then you ask if he is satisfied with your performance. If this is the case, you can now even ask for paid extra days.

3.1.16 Anchoring

Anchoring a modern and effective method of manipulation that comes from psychology involves working with a trigger. This is usually a word that is very special and is especially emphasized. However, it can also be a certain value, which is then unconsciously taken as a reference. Anchoring works subconsciously, and we can hardly escape this mechanism. It is very often used in restaurants, but also in private negotiations.

Application Example:

You want to sell your used car, so that you get as much as possible, you take a price that is at the top of the usual range. Because there are no clear prices for used cars, you anchor a price on which a buyer can orientate himself. He must now bid on this price, although the actual value is much lower.

3.1.17 Priming

When priming or vaccinating, we try to bring certain words into the memory of the other person without him noticing. The next step is to recall these words, albeit in a different context. The psychological background is that we usually only remember the last thing that was said in a certain context - or rather, what we last heard has a higher quality in memory. You may know the party game where you are asked what color clouds have, what color a goal line has, what color a doctor's coat has. All answers are "white". If you are then asked what the cow is drinking, you will probably say milk because your brain is trying to figure out what the recent memory has to do with a cow. It looks for a drink and associates it with the color white. However, priming usually only works for short periods of time.

Application Example:

If you know that your boss has to write a review about you, you can send him a text beforehand, in which, for example, the expression "excellent team player" appears. He will then unconsciously use what he saw last.

3.1.18 Halo-Effect

The halo or halo effect refers to the first impression we get of someone. This means that what we first see of someone outshines everything else. For example, we always have negative associations with dirty beggars, but we are open to a properly dressed and polite person, even if he wants to cheat us. The old saying "first impression counts" is indeed based on psychological studies, and you can't really avoid it. But of course, you can use this effect to manipulate others.

Application Example:

You want a loan from the bank. You have securities, but maybe not enough, and therefore, you want to talk to a bank employee. Put on a good suit or business dress, clean shoes and dark socks or pantyhose. You should be shaved/haired properly. It is also helpful to enter the room with a friendly smile. Even if you later show a different side in the conversation, your counterpart will have a hard time overwriting the first impression.

3.1.19 Scarcity

You can best manipulate people when they're pressurized. We try to avoid pressure, it's a natural reaction. And especially psychological pressure works very well. The scarcity method is often used to put pressure on a buyer. It is particularly successful when someone has already decided on a model. Then you can tell him that there is only one piece left in stock, and at least three are sold per day. The buyer is now under pressure, he knows he has to make the decision now. It doesn't matter anymore that other stores might still have some products in stock.

Application Example:

A discount alone does not always help to sell remaining stock. However, what has proven its worth are the so-called rummage tables. Goods are placed randomly on a table. The buyer knows that discounts are only available for products that are still on the table. This increases the pressure to strike now, because otherwise, you will miss the bargain.

3.1.20 Disqualification

When it comes to selling more to a customer than he can afford (or is willing to spend), this method may seem a little mean, but it is also very effective. It also works in other situations, especially in relationships and friendships. What you do is tell the other person that they can't afford something and thus disqualify themselves.

Application Example:

You want to organize a party with friends and they think beer and cola are enough. But at least you want to have some more schnapps. Instead of telling them what you want, you pretend to make a list of possible drinks, and then casually say that tequila is really good for the party, but probably too expensive for your friends. You can even suggest buying a bottle yourself, but it would look embarrassing if there was only one bottle of tequila.

3.1.21 Blatancy

In the same direction as with the listing of precise facts, although somewhat more general, the obviousness tactic goes. Here, no facts are presented, but common sense. Just as facts cannot be checked at short notice, obvious arguments cannot simply be ignored. In this tactic, rhetorical questions are rather asked, or even only a statement is given. It is important that your argument is also obvious to your counterpart.

Application Example:

You want to sell a customer a new phone. He actually wants a cheap model, but you want to sell him an iPhone. Sentences like "Everyone knows Apple phones are not only safer, they last longer," "It's obvious a cheap phone also has a bad battery that lasts a few hours," or "It's common knowledge Android phones are unsafe because they don't get updates."

3.1.22 Word of Honor

A somewhat personal method is the word of honour method. Here, you should at least have established some kind of personal relationship with your counterpart, even if it is through a somewhat longer sales talk. If you feel that facts or authority do not help, the Word of Honour is a perfect way to put the other person under pressure to make a decision. If someone gives you a word of honor, he will hardly lie - at least that's what we think. It doesn't really have to be an oath, milder forms like a promise or an insurance do. Even if the word of honour has a lot to do with honour, it is often broken enough. It is up to you when you want to use it.

Application Example:

You've been checking Facebook at work to see what your friends are doing, and your boss suspects you're not working enough. But he can't prove it. If you now tell him that you assure him that work is always the highest priority and give him your word of honour that nothing is more important, he will most likely refrain from other investigations - even if he still suspects you. He has to bring evidence against a word of honor and if he doesn't, he has to back down.

3.1.23 The loser

This strategy is actually a kind of anti-dominance method. Because here, you do not show the other your superiority, but inferiority. But because you only use it to manipulate someone, in the end, you gain dominance again. This is about giving your counterpart the feeling of being so much better than yourself. Women like to play this game when they say they don't know anything about computers and men when they have to cook. The method works similar to the compliment method, but it is reinforced by the fact that we seem to go to a low position while at the same time raising the other's position.

Application Example:

You want to sell a customer a camera that is expensive, but also has a lot of features. Instead of explaining all the features to the customer, you let him play with the camera first and praise him for every feature he tries, and says you can't do it yourself. You can even take it to the extreme and ask him how he just did it. He will feel so superior that it might be quite easy to let him buy the camera. Especially if instead of "Do you want to buy the camera now?" you ask him what other accessories he needs, maybe another lens or a spare battery.

3.1.24 The raised index finger

Almost everything we do consciously is done within the framework of our values. We check actions and reactions, whether they are good or bad. Sometimes, we throw this overboard, for example, when we get in the car after three beers or when we smoke. But morality is important for us, and you can make people follow you by pointing out moral reasons, even if they are not necessarily willing to do so - as long as your offer does not contradict their moral ideas. Often, environmental issues are suitable, or healthy nutrition, but also humanity in general.

Application Example:

You want to sell a new desk to a customer, but it is much more expensive than a normal model because it is made of certified tropical wood. The customer doesn't care about the wood at first, mainly because he has to pay more for it. Then you explain to him that this wood secures the habitat of jungle dwellers and great apes, and that if more people buy such wood, fewer orangutans have to die.

3.1.25 Chess Method: Thinking One Step Ahead

If you have some experience in sales talks, but also in discussions in general, then you can try to predict what your counterpart wants to say next, as in chess, and invalidate that already before. This will unsettle your opponent, because you will disarm him.

Application Example:

You want to buy a new sofa, but you know that your partner is against it. To convince your partner, think about what counter arguments you can come up with: For example, too expensive, the old sofa is still good, there are more important things to buy, money must be saved. Now, try to find suitable counter arguments. When it then comes to the conversation, you immediately fire all concerns and your comments on it, and can so push your partner into the corner that he follows your wish.

3.1.26 Three alternatives trick

One of the most popular tricks of sellers are the three alternatives. A selection is presented to the customer, but it is designed in such a way that he actually has only one choice. Often, an alternative C is so expensive or so bad that it fails from the outset. The other two alternatives A and B are actually more expensive than what the customer wanted. But after he has already made a decision that he only has to choose between A and B, and that he no longer has the idea of wanting anything else. This strategy also works in professional life if you want to push through an idea in a meeting. The advantage is that the manipulated person has the feeling that he has made a decision himself.

Application Example:

You should create a new website for your company. You yourself have a great idea, but you know that your boss always wants to make his own decision. So you create one version that you know he will reject, and then two versions that differ only slightly and essentially follow your suggestion.

3.1.27 The foot in the door

Sometimes, you can't just fall into the house with the door, but have to have only one foot in the door to stay in the picture. With this method, you will first ask for a small concession. Representatives did not say the saying "Do you have some time?" at the front door for nothing, because then those asked for a "yes" were more willing to make further concessions. The same applies to small favours that precede larger favours, for example if you want a colleague to take over the weekend shift. First, he is asked if he can take over the phone for a moment. This technique is often followed by the yes-street.

Application Example:
You want to sell a subscription on the phone. You call a customer and ask if you can ask a few questions for a survey. After these are asked, you can ask if he or she already has a similar subscription.

3.2 Manipulation based on instincts

Instincts are behaviours that are deeply anchored in our brain, and that we cannot control or can only control to a certain extent. They are primordial behaviours that have ensured the survival of our species. Our instincts have proven themselves and that is why they are so deep in our brains. Even in the language this still shows up: We "smell danger". We "tremble with fear". One can consciously address these instincts and trigger them in a person if one wants to manipulate him.

3.2.1 Herd Instinct

Basically, man is a herd animal. This is a primal instinct that offers us security. We like to follow the masses - similar to the legendary lemmings. That's why we stop at a crowd in an accident, and at a street musician who already has an audience. Hat players push this technique to the top, but in the crowd, the alleged passers-by are their own people. Good salespeople often refer to other customers who have also bought this product. This also works in the relationship: "The others also go to the concert". We find experiences that other people have had with a fact, a product or a service to be valuable hints for our own opinion-forming and purchasing decisions. This principle is used above all by advertising. Again and again we hear and read that millions of people have already been inspired by a certain product or service - at this point, it remains to be seen; whether this is really true or not, according to the motto "Do not trust any statistics that you have not falsified yourself".

Application Example:
A customer wants to buy a television, but is not sure which model he wants. After the seller knows the price range, he proposes a Model X. To make it more palatable, he shows the customer reviews on a consumer platform on the Internet.

Everyday/practical examples:

<u>Case 1:</u>

"93 percent of users were very satisfied with the XYZ product."

"Of course, I am one of the 93 percent of these users. After all, I want to be a part of it, and not an obstructionist driver."

"If so many people were satisfied with the product, I'm sure I will be."

These are typical thoughts or emotions, which the advertisement in you would like to trigger. If so many people are of the same opinion, then you certainly do not want to be outside and belong to this group of people. By the way, you are not alone with this, because only very few people are strong enough to stand against a majority of opinions.

This form of manipulation is therefore one of the most effective manipulation techniques available. Above all, people with weak opinions are subject to the temptation to let this strategy force them to make a certain decision.

<u>Case 2:</u>

> "Why can't I have a cell phone? All the other kids in my class already have one."

Children in particular are true masters at using the trick of the crowd to their advantage, and manipulating their parents to make their wishes come true. As a parent, you'd rather fulfil your child's desire for a mobile phone if all the other children supposedly already own a smartphone. As I said, man is a herd animal, and you certainly don't want to expect your child to be an "outsider". However, it is often forgotten that a certain product or opinion is not automatically meaningful or recommendable, just because the majority allegedly holds this opinion or owns this product.

3.2.2 Reciprocity

We have been taught from childhood to show gratitude for a favor with a counter favor. "I owe you something" is often the answer when someone has done us a favor. In business, you can take advantage of that to get people to return a favor with a purchase. The effect is deeply rooted in us. You can also observe it in animals. So, chimpanzees let other chimpanzees come to eat if they had offered the same before. There are even theories that this altruism also had advantages in reproduction, and has therefore remained a form of behaviour for so long. This also explains why we consciously cannot resist it.

Application Example:

The supermarket sells meat loaf. To boost sales, a table is set up in front of the meat counter where a salesman stands and offers tasting pieces to customers. The customer is happy to have received something as a gift, and we are more willing to buy a piece of meat cheese, even if it is not on our shopping list.

3.2.3 Ask for help

As social beings, we have learned that we should help other people. This can be excellently exploited in communication to get something that the other person may not necessarily want to give away. Cries for help always trigger a helper syndrome in us. This is quasi part of our DNA. Mothers are alarmed when the baby screams, even in the animal world it is so. The help manipulation technique is based on this basic instinct.

Application Example:

You hate to mow the grass in the garden, but then, it's too high. You go to your neighbour and ask him if he can help you, possibly pointing to a sore back. If he has time, he will hardly be able to deny you help. Attention: You should not overdo it with this technique, at some point, your neighbour will see through you.

3.2.4 Anxiety and Relief

This technique belongs to the rather "bad" manipulation strategies, but it also works excellently. It is about playing with each other's feelings and scaring them. You have to make the other feel so much fear (or stress) that he would accept any help to get out of this situation. And this is exactly what you offer him. With the relief, the other loses the ability to make rational decisions for a short time, and is more likely to agree to suggestions. Here, too, the basis of human history can be seen. Especially in the early days the hunters were under constant stress: Wild animals, searching for food and protecting themselves from enemies determined everyday life. They were all the more pleased when the stress was taken away from them.

Application Example:

An employee who is actually good, but has been a little unfocused lately, has to come to you because he won't get the salary increase that's actually due. You explain to him that the company has to see which good employees it can keep and that dismissals cannot be ruled out. In addition to competence, performance is also a prerequisite for keeping the job, and this leaves a lot to be desired. He first has to wait for a salary increase. The employee will now be so afraid that you can make it easier for him to keep the job that he will agree to it.

3.2.5 Hunter-gatherer method

Instincts of prehistoric man are still present in us. We cannot deny the hunter in us or the collector. You can take advantage of this by giving others the opportunity to hunt or collect something. In marketing, coupons are often used, in coffee shops, there are bonus cards. In relationships, you can appeal to the hunter in men - they will hardly let an easy prey go.

Application Example:

You are an investment broker and want to sell a certain fund. General performance values are good and beautiful, and so is the portfolio, but ultimately, the client wants a loot. So if you work with concrete numbers, the customer has an idea and can "go hunting". It is better, for example, to say "If this fund performs as before, then you will make a profit of 2000 euros with your investment in one year. You don't want to miss out on something like that, do you?

3.2.6 Sex

An old advertising slogan is "Sex sells", and there is something to it - which, by the way, applies to both sexes. While top models are usually used in advertising, many companies take good-looking employees with them to sales talks, even if they are not involved in the actual conversation. If you train regularly as a man, then a tight-fitting shirt can work wonders for women (but also for men) and short skirts and a low neckline are also still an eye-catcher. The point is not to reduce one person to one object, but to manipulate another. If his attention is on the breasts or chest muscles, then he or she shows an open flank that you can exploit.

Application Example:

From Asia, you can learn how to influence a man to make a decision. There, it is common to invite business partners and friends to bars where they are served by very handsome women. So if you go to such a bar with a business partner and enjoy some beer and the presence of some ladies with him, then he will be very inclined to accept your suggestion - especially if he gets a reward for a "yes", for example to spend time with the lady of his choice. It also works for women; you only have to look at the Chippendales audience once.

4. How can you tell you're being manipulated?

4.1 Manipulative people like to listen to you

A manipulative person wants to hear what you have to say. Why? In this way, he can easily recognize your strengths and weaknesses. He will first ask you a few questions so that you can talk about your emotions and personal opinions. The manipulator introduces such questions with "Why", "How" or "What". The following actions and answers of the manipulator are then based on the information you have given him.

If someone lets you speak first, this is of course not an attempt at manipulation in itself, but can also be a sign of politeness. It is important that you also observe the other actions of the person:

- A manipulator hardly reveals any personal information during the conversation itself, and instead concentrates on getting as much of this information as possible from you.

- If this person shows such behaviour again and again in conversations with you, this can be a sign for manipulation.

- Even if the other person's interest seems authentic, be careful, because behind his questions, there might be a hidden intention. Test the true motivations of your counterpart by asking him questions. If he doesn't respond or changes the subject quickly, it's usually not real interest.

4.2 Manipulative people use all their charm

To achieve their goals, manipulative people use the full range of their charms. So, a manipulative person compliments you on many things before he asks you for a favor. Maybe he will give you a small gift or a card before he comes out with his request. The manipulation attempt is quite obvious if he promises to do you a favor if you grant him his request.

This manipulation tactic is closely connected with the motto "One hand washes the other". In a collegial framework, this is actually okay. However, manipulative people also like to use this method in their private environment, for example, to influence their friends and acquaintances. Women also like to use their female charms with the aim to get a certain wish fulfilled - just think of waiters in the restaurant who serve your food and drinks with a sweeping décolleté. Surely, you as a man are more inclined in this case to give a generous tip. So in this case, the waitress has used her charm and her feminine charms to top up her tip.

4.3 Manipulators use apparent facts

Just because the person you are talking to is "banging your ears" with all kinds of facts does not mean that these facts are objectively true. So, you would do well to check the correctness of facts that are mentioned in a conversation before you let them count.

Manipulators like to use some facts and dubious information to manipulate you. Such facts can be manipulated by lying or deliberately withholding certain information or exaggerating. Some manipulators pretend to be true experts in a certain field and bombard you with statistics and facts. On the one hand, these facts do not necessarily have to correspond to the truth, and on the other hand, such people want to feel more powerful than you, according to the motto "knowledge is power".

For the manipulator, it doesn't matter if his facts are completely out of context or if the information mentioned is valid at all.

Best examples for the attempt of the manipulation with the help of facts are some postings in social networks, which gladly pursue the goal of fuelling fear or social envy with the population. Also, some dubious profit plays use this manipulation tactic and set completely on the greed of the users.

4.4 Bathe in self-pity

Maybe you also have one or the other person in your environment who likes to see himself as a victim and who plays the martyr again and again.

This procedure basically has two manipulative goals:

(1) On the one hand, people like to do this in order to be the focus of attention, true to the motto "envy is something you have to work hard for, pity is a gift".

(2) On the other hand, manipulators who like to see themselves as victims will do you some favors in the beginning, which you didn't ask for. However, they still expect you to return the favor. If you do not do this, they will complain and want to make you feel guilty.

Manipulative people who use self-pity tactics like to complain that no one loves them, that they are always sick, and that they are always the victim. They want to increase the probability that you will help them to get their lives under control, and in addition, they are using their behavior to solicit affection and sympathy.

4.5 Check if the friendliness is genuine

You may have a friend or acquaintance who can be very nice to you - if you do what he wants you to do, or if you have completed a required task to his satisfaction. Conversely, if you refuse him a favor, he will "punish" you with outbursts of anger, ignorance or other negative behaviors.

Such manipulators have two faces:

- an angelic face if he wants to be liked by you

- a horrible face if he wants you to be afraid of him.

The relationship between you two always seems to be in perfect order until you fail to live up to his expectations and fail in his eyes.

For you, this means a permanent change on the narrow ridge, a walk on raw eggs, always in fear of annoying him.

4.6 Pay attention to certain patterns of behaviour

Every person is manipulative from time to time, because we all strive to see our needs and desires fulfilled. A real manipulator, however, almost always shows corresponding manipulative behavior patterns. He pursues a personal plan and tries to exploit other people with full intention. Why? At the expense of other people, a manipulator strives for more control, power and privilege.

If you should notice this behavior regularly with a person in your environment, you can be relatively sure that you are dealing with a real manipulator.

How do you feel if you feel manipulated by a human being again and again? Your rights and interests are often denied or minimized, and do not seem to play a big role for the manipulator, because **HIS** wishes, needs and goals are at the top of his list. Him first, before everyone else later.

But beware: the described behaviour can also be shown by people who suffer from depression or other mental illnesses. These illnesses mean that the affected person feels guilty, but does not have the real intention to consciously manipulate you and use you for his own benefit.

4.7 Are you being judged?

If you have the feeling that a person makes fun of you again and again, or "hacks" at you, then this is a clear sign that this person wants to manipulate you. His goal is to make you feel inadequate. He achieves this through statements or behaviour that makes you feel you can never please him; everything you do is not good enough for him.

Such a manipulator will mainly pick out the negative things, and not offer you helpful suggestions or constructive criticism. So, he will not support you in correcting the "mistakes" he has put forward, but will be graciously showing you off.

This behaviour becomes particularly drastic when you are shown off by means of jokes or sarcasm. A manipulative person might like to make jokes about your car, your family, your workplace or your clothes. This will lead to insecurity and a bad feeling in you. Your counterpart has then managed to manipulate your self-esteem. His goal may be that you try to compensate for this lack of self-esteem with actions that are useful to the manipulator in some way. He wants to arouse in you the feeling that you want to prove to him that you can do, or represent more than he believes you can do in his statements.

4.8 Silence as a punishment?

In order to exercise control, some manipulative people use silence. This is done, for example, by ignoring calls, e-mails or other messages over a longer period of time. The goal of this manipulation strategy is to unsettle you, or to show you that you have done something wrong. The manipulator is in control in this case, and you may worry about what mistake you might have made.

For example, if you are a relationship type who likes to live in harmony with others, this manipulation tactic will work very well for you. It may not even be necessary for you to have made a concrete mistake - a manipulative person also likes to use this strategy to simply exercise power over other people.

If you then speak to this person about the reasons for his silence, he may deny that something is wrong, or tell you that you are reacting illogically or paranoid. These answers in turn lead to further uncertainty, because you may now also doubt the objectivity of your perception.

4.9 Do you have to apologize all the time?

Some manipulative people are able to turn certain situations into the opposite in an ingenious way. Again, you may get the feeling that YOU have done something wrong, even if objectively this is not the case. For example, this can happen if you are accused of something you did not do, or are held responsible for a certain situation.

For example, if you date a person at a certain time, and that person appears much later than you did, you may be irritated to confront them. Instead of apologizing to you, which would be appropriate for the situation, a manipulative person tries to make you feel guilty. This happens, for example, with a statement like:

"Yes, of course, I never do anything right. It's a miracle you still talk to me anyway, because I'm always to blame for everything."

Through such statements, a manipulative person turns the nature of the conversation around and makes you feel compassion or sympathy for them. You now have the feeling that you have to apologize to the manipulator for your complaint, even if objectively, this would not be your job at all, because an apology would have to come from the manipulative person much sooner.

4.10 You are being compared

When a person constantly compares you to other people, they probably want to persuade you to do a certain action or behavior. Her argument is that all other people would have no problem with this action or behavior. She may even list these people's names or make you understand that their friends or partners would do it. She may add the threat that you may look stupid if you do not do this action or behavior. The purpose of the manipulator is to make you feel guilty. For this purpose, the manipulative human builds up pressure and exerts it on you.

Example:

"Erik and Marie have already gone on holiday twice this year. Only we don't do that."

If your partner confronts you with this statement, you will automatically be pushed into a position where you have to justify yourself - regardless of the reasons why you have not gone on holiday with your partner twice this year. Through this comparison with friends or acquaintances, your partner tries to manipulate you, to give in to his wish and to go on holiday with him. Possible consequences or lack of money do not matter to him in this case.

5. Don't become a victim - proven defense techniques against manipulations

5.1. Ignore and continue

Surely this defense technique is an extremely cautious reaction if you recognize a manipulation technique in a conversation. When ignoring and continuing, you simply don't even go into the manipulation attempt and ignore the statement in question. In this way, you can warn your interlocutor without him losing face.

It is important, however, that you let your manipulative interlocutor know that you did notice that he tried to manipulate the conversation.

This happens for example through:

- a targeted pause in a conversation,

- a question like, "Are you okay with us going back to this?"

- a particularly constructive contribution from you.

Everyday/practical examples:

<u>Case 1:</u>
You are in a lively discussion with a human being. In the beginning your conversation, your partner is still

discussing very constructively with you. At some point, however, he seems to run out of arguments and is emphatically disinterested and bored.

With the defense technique Ignore and continue, you could ask your interlocutor if he can still follow you, and which arguments he would like to put forward. In this way, you signal to him that you have seen through his manipulative behavior and at the same time, you ask him in a constructive and charming way to get involved again in the discussion with you.

Case 2:
Your partner reproaches you - whether these are justified or not. or what the reason for these reproaches is, does not matter at this point. You discuss with each other and suddenly, your partner makes a stupid joke or a cynical remark about you.

In this case, you should not go to the same level as your partner, but try to put the conversation back on a factual basis. This can be done, for example, by telling your partner that you are interested in a factual and constructive solution to the problem. Hereby, you indicate that you have taken note of his cynical remark, but do not want to enter this level. You note that you would rather talk to your partner objectively and neutrally.

5.2 Play dumb

Maybe you know the proverb "The fox is smart and poses stupid..." You can use this idiom when you talk to a manipulative person.

If you act stupid in this conversation, you may react to the manipulation attempt, but you officially interpret it as a misunderstanding and a little confusion. Before you can continue the conversation, this confusion must be removed or the misunderstanding cleared up. In this way, you can avoid making your conversation partner look like a manipulator. He can then save his face, and at the same time has experienced a very elegant warning signal from you.

Everyday/practical example
You are in the middle of a conflict with a friend. In order to solve this conflict, you both agreed that everyone should first present and explain their point of view. Your interlocutor didn't keep to this agreement and didn't even present his point of view, but conjured his proposed solution out of his hat.

You can now act stupid in this situation and put your interlocutor in his place, for example by saying: "Please wait a moment; I am a bit confused right now. Shortly before, we had both agreed to first present our points of view. But you had already offered me a solution before. Should this be an example or was it an anticipation?"

5.3 Record with a crack

If you notice that your interviewer wants to distract from the topic, or wants to make you feel attacked, irritated or intimidated, it can be helpful to play the record with a jump. To do this, you repeat in the conversation again and again very persistently what is important to you, what matters to you, what you want or what you want to ask.

Important note: The record with jump requires a lot of practice - like all other conversation techniques. Why? Already from childhood, we learn that stubbornness and directness are not desired in a conversation. However, the record with jump as a tool against manipulation tactics is morally impeccable, because nobody is devalued, disregarded or deceived by this. You only make use of your right to say what you want or what is important to you on a record with a jump.

Everyday/practical example:
You are in a discussion with your partner. You want to make him aware of a mistake he made. During the conversation, he tries again and again to distract you from this topic and to open up secondary war scenes.

This is the ideal opportunity for you to put on the record with a jump in order to ward off your partner's manipulation attempts. If your partner tries to distract from the actual topic, then answer him that you are willing to talk to him about this topic, if you have found a solution to your topic before. By doing so, you signal to him that his topics are important to him, but that you have addressed your topic first, and would like to continue this discussion before devoting yourself to your partner's topic.

5.4 Changing the perspective

This defense against manipulation attempts is basically very simple. With this protection technique, you do not respond directly to the manipulation attempt, but invite your interlocutor to see the situation with your eyes, or with the eyes of a third person. During the conversation, you consciously change the perspective.

Everyday/practical example:
You and your partner have a little argument in which you have to listen to all kinds of reproaches. Perhaps, your partner also expresses if-then-expressions in order to put you under pressure - thus quite clearly, a typical manipulation attempt. Instead of feeling pushed into a corner, you can defuse the situation by responding to your partner: "XYZ, your utterance confuses / hurts me now. Please put yourself in my position / How do you think I feel about your statement now".

Through this statement, you set a clear stop signal and at the same time give your partner the opportunity to reflect on what he has said. You also prevent an escalation of the conversation and give your partner the opportunity to see the situation with your eyes.

A change of perspective is ideally suited in conversations in which your conversation partner stubbornly poses or pretends not to understand your statements. A change of perspective is also useful if your interviewer insists on his point of view and almost "digs himself" into his position.

5.5 Step out of the situation

In some cases, the best solution is to ward off manipulation techniques by literally "grabbing the bull by the horns". For this purpose, you interrupt the conversation resolutely and openly address the manipulation attempt of your interlocutor. You do not necessarily have to do this with the wooden hammer method, but can do it elegantly with the following procedure:

(1) First, interrupt the conversation clearly and unambiguously.

(2) Then explain this interruption briefly and concisely.

(3) Ask the question in the room how it can/should go on now.

Everyday/practical example:

In a conversation, your partner expresses himself which is insulting to you. This is a particularly drastic manipulation attempt. At this point of the conversation, it is now up to you to set a stop signal. This happens for example with the statement "At this point, I do not want to talk further, because I do not want to be insulted. I would like us to be able to resume our conversation on a factual level. Do you agree with that?

In this example, after attempting to manipulate (insult) your counterpart, you clearly interrupted the conversation (" at this point, I don't want to talk any more") and explained to your interlocutor why you did this ("I don't want to be insulted."). At the same time, however, you also offer your counterpart the opportunity to continue the conversation ("I want us to be able to continue our conversation on a factual level again"). Do you agree with that?") and are you very fair to him with it.

The key point of this defense technique is to directly address and identify the manipulation attempt. Before you do this, however, you should clearly interrupt the conversation beforehand. Why? This is important in order not to mix the factual level of the conversation with the relationship level of your counterpart. If you do not make this separation clear enough, it can lead to the content of the conversation and the subsequent question of how to deal with each other in the conversation, and becoming mixed up in such a way that neither you nor your counterpart can recognize what it is actually about.

5.6 How to deal with blockages

It is not uncommon to find yourself in a "dead end" in a conversation. This happens because your conversation partner is bricking up and trying to block the conversation. The following escalation model provides a remedy for this. In this model, different phases and steps are described with which you can react to a blockade of your conversation partner. The methods and means you use become clearer and more direct from phase to phase.

Method:

    (1) Understanding of the interlocutor

    (2) Accuse the counterpart of cooperation

    (3) Signaling willingness to cooperate to the interlocutor

    (4) Open blockade address

    (5) Using power fairly

Phase 1: Understanding the interlocutor

You have noticed the blockade of your interlocutor and are now trying to understand his situation. During this phase you should above all listen and ask (as open as possible) questions. Your goal in this phase should be to find out the needs and possible fears of your counterpart.

Phase 2: Assigning cooperation to the counterpart

Even if your conversation partner should continue to build a wall, first believe in the good in people and assume they are willing to cooperate. There are three recommended ways to do this:

- Ignore and continue (see also chapter 5.1):

    "All right, let's keep talking about our subject. First, I want to bring you my point of view."

- Stupid (see also chapter 5.1):

    "One thing is still not quite clear to me. Surely I did not express myself correctly."

- Interpret the behaviour of the other person positively:

    "Because you don't want to answer my question, I think you have an important reason. So I withdraw my question."

Phase 3: Signaling willingness to cooperate with your partner

During this phase, you can now try to signal your willingness to cooperate to your interlocutor. The best way to do this is to take the first step.

"I notice you don't seem to want to share your interests immediately. Is it okay with you if I take this first step?"

If the blockade has not been resolved by then, we will move on to the fourth phase.

Phase 4: Address the blockade openly

In this phase, the defense method "Step out of the situation" is used. So you interrupt the conversation and address the blockade of your counterpart directly. You can formulate this as follows:

> *"I'd like to interrupt this conversation at this point. You have not yet answered any of my questions, and have not made any suggestions as to what you think we can do. To be honest, I have the impression that you are building a wall. Why do you do that?"*

If you don't make any progress in the fourth phase, you enter phase 5.

Phase 5: Using Power in a Fair Way

In order to be able to use your power fairly, you must first find out what your power is in relation to your interlocutor. The power you can then use in a conversation is your exit option. This determines what you do if the conversation with your interlocutor should fail. Therefore, it makes sense to ask yourself before the conversation how you would like to proceed if the conversation should fail. It is important that you remain fair. In this context, fair means that you announce what you are doing to your interviewer, and at the same time, give him the opportunity to come back to a result-oriented and objective conversation. Ideally, you should follow the following **three steps:**

(1) **Announce your intention as a fair offer.**

(2) **Use your power clearly and reasoned.**

(3) **Trade consistent with this rationale.**

What are the advantages of fair use of power?
On the one hand, you give the manipulator the opportunity to get back into a solution-oriented and objective dialogue. On the other hand, you also make it clear to him what consequences he has to expect if he does not respond to your offer. So, you don't just threaten him with a sanction, but give him a free choice. So, he himself can decide whether he wants to finish the conversation on a factual level or live with the consequences of his manipulative conversational behaviour.

5.7 How to interrupt a conversation

It is sad, but unfortunately the truth: Sometimes, there is no other way than to break off a conversation clearly and unambiguously. This is important in order to protect oneself on the one hand, and to pull oneself out of the affair as elegantly as possible on the other. Among the widespread, however less elegant possibilities to break off a discussion there are:

⇓ Reproach the interviewer,

⇓ make concrete or vague threats,

⇓ swear, scold and retreat

⇓ to blame the other person for the unsuccessful conversation,

⇓ swallowing any anger that may have arisen during the conversation,

⇓ ditching your interlocutors

⇓ leave the termination of the conversation to the other party.

But how can a conversation be broken off stylishly and gently? In these situations, you should try the following if possible:

⇑ Break off the conversation yourself, because that's how you keep the initiative.

⇑ Tell the other person clearly the reasons for the interruption of the conversation.

⇑ Alert the call partner to the consequences of the call interruption.

Everyday/practical example:

You're in a conflict with a friend. Your counterpart deviates more and more from the actual topic, and all attempts on your part to bring the conversation back to an objective level fail. You have already announced to your friend that you will end the conversation if the two of you cannot return to an objective level, but even this announced sanction has not borne fruit in the conversation. For this reason, you now have no choice but to end the conversation. This can happen, for example, through the following statement:

"Unfortunately, I have the feeling that we're not getting anywhere at this point. I hate to do it, but the conversation is over for me after your behaviour. I would like to discuss with you on a factual level, but at the moment, this is obviously not possible. I would like to offer you that we meet again tomorrow at XY o'clock to continue the conversation."

In this example, you have made it clear to your interviewer why you want to end the conversation. At the same time, however, you made him an offer to continue the conversation the next day. You have thus signalled a basic willingness on your part to continue the conversation. Whether he finally accepts this offer or not is of course not up to you, but depends on the person you are talking to.

An interruption of a conversation is the "worst case" in communication, i.e. the worst of all possible cases. But you should also take such unpleasant situations into account and be sufficiently prepared for them, because even in this case, it is ultimately a matter of protecting yourself.

6. False arguments and how you can defend yourself against them

It is in a person's nature to want to assert oneself in discussions, negotiations or conversations. In order to achieve this goal, we also like to use manipulative methods. However, you should keep in mind that these manipulation traps are often used unconsciously. In some cases, we use false arguments without really being aware of it. If we can identify false arguments in a conversation, we have taken the first step towards a better way of argumentation.

But what false arguments and argumentation traps are there, and how can you successfully defend yourself against them in a conversation?

6.1 General Tips for Defense

There are various ways in which you can defend yourself against fake arguments and tricks of argumentation. For each of the manipulation attempts listed later, you will experience a concrete defense possibility.

Irrespective of the respective argumentation trick or sham argument, however, it makes sense to take the following steps:

First step: Recognize the tactics and identify mistakes

This first step is often the decisive point in dealing with pseudo-arguments and argumentation tricks, because if you realize that a trap has been set up by your conversation partner, you will not blindly step into it. It is often problematic that you do not even notice that you have just fallen victim to a false argumentation. Only when you know which tactic your opponent is using can you identify the central weak point of this manipulation attempt and initiate counter measures.

Second step: Initiate fair counter measures

There are a number of different counter measures that you can use to counter manipulation attempts in a fair way.

a) You can directly address the mistake your conversation partner makes, or the tactics he uses to manipulate the conversation. You can call the manipulation attempt of your interlocutor directly by name. Often, the concrete naming of the applied manipulation tactic leads to a frightened trying to outwit or stunned pausing of the manipulator. He will most likely not use the tactic in conversations with you again in the future.

b) You can ask critical questions about the argumentation of the manipulator. These questions expose central weak points of the argumentation trap. Especially elegant in this context, are critical questions in a friendly tone.

c) You can demand real justifications from the manipulator for their conversational behaviour. Apparent arguments are often used by people to pretend that they have sufficient reasoning. His goal is to convince you of a different point of view. But if you demand real reasons from your counterpart, you make it clear to him that you have seen through his tactics, and he is now in the burden of proof to give you true reasons.

6.2 What are the most popular pseudo-arguments and argumentation traps?

6.2.1. Black-and-white painting
Black and white painting is one of the most effective manipulation manoeuvres, as it gives the impression of logical reasoning. In black and white painting, the manipulator uses either or arguments:

*"**Either** we go on vacation to the mountains or to the sea"*

This means that if you don't want to go to the sea, your holiday will automatically lead to the mountains or vice versa. So, there are **only two options** for this form of argumentation. If case A does not occur, case B occurs and vice versa. Basically, this argumentation is logical in itself. In everyday discussions, however, a fatal error becomes obvious here. This way of argumentation secretly presupposes that only the two given alternatives exist. Only if this is the case, the argument can actually be valid.

Example:
In a television show, a candidate stands in front of two doors, and is supposed to decide between one of the two - either door A or door B.

In this case, the reasoning is absolutely correct because there are only two alternatives.

But what about the question of the holiday destination? Are there really only the two possibilities to go to the sea or to the mountains? No, certainly not, a holiday in other regions is also conceivable in principle.

So the manipulator uses the black and white painting in this case to exert a logical pressure on you with the aim to join his argumentation.

How can you defend yourself?
If you are confronted with such an argumentation, it is best to ask yourself immediately whether the assertion of your counterpart really contains all alternatives. If you limit yourself to only two possible alternatives through either- or statements, you promote black-and-white thinking and block independent further thinking. It only takes a little imagination from you to break through this blockade, because in very few cases, you will have only two mutually exclusive options.

In the example mentioned at the beginning, the question was whether you should spend your holidays with your partner in the mountains or by the sea.

In order to defend yourself against this argumentation trap, it is best to ask your partner critically why only these two options are available, and whether there is not yet a third or fourth alternative. You put your opponent in the position of having to logically justify his trap of argumentation, which in most cases will be difficult for him to succeed. If he has no good reasons why he only offers two holiday destinations to choose from, you can now suggest more holiday destinations that you are interested in.

6.2.2 Black dyeing

It is common argumentation to point out the negative consequences of a position or a point of view. These consequences are not desirable. For this reason, it is argued that it is necessary to reject the original position.

Everyday/practical example

You have a well-paid job, but you don't enjoy it. For this reason, you would like to start studying and then work in another profession.

In a conversation with your partner, he or she will tell you that he or she is not enthusiastic about this idea. He paints you in the most dazzling - actually rather darkest - colours, what financial loss this decision would entail for you.

This example clearly shows that it is difficult for you to assert your position against your partner, i.e. your desire for a professional change and the associated studies. He paints out for you the drastic consequences that your decision - in his opinion - would bring for both of you. So, if you decide to reorient your career, it would have serious consequences that you both would have to suffer.

In this example, your partner tries to manipulate you by taking your position and drawing a picture of the dark and drastic consequences of your position. Your partner hopes to intimidate you so much that you withdraw from your position.

How can you now defend yourself against black dyeing?
Three techniques have proven their worth as defense against this attempt at manipulation:

(1) You can name the tactic you have exposed directly, and in this way, make your partner aware that you are being manipulated by him. It is possible that your partner will be forced to defuse his assessment of the consequences, as he will notice that his description is a bit too dramatic.

(2) You can counter your partner by saying that the consequences he mentions do not necessarily follow from your decision to reorient your career. For example, you may receive financial support from the state or your family during your studies.

(3) In some cases, the consequences are clearly too radical to really become reality. In addition, the manipulator in black dyeing often tries to portray the consequences as irrevocable consequences. Why? He wants to give his argument the necessary strength.

(4) You can counteract the tactics of black coloring by showing positive consequences resulting from your position. In the above example, this would include more enjoyment of your work, possible career opportunities and a higher income in the long run. Under certain circumstances, these positive consequences outweigh - ultimately not only for you, but also in the eyes of your partner.

6.2.3 Avalanche arguments

Avalanche arguments are part of slide tactics. Also, in this case, your opponent points out negative consequences. Why is this manipulation attempt called "slide tactic"? Imagine you take the first step on a slide. A short time later, there is no stopping and you can no longer control the situation.

This is another reason why avalanche arguments are often used in slide tactics. The triggering of avalanches happens by small carelessness. An avalanche begins very gently, as a small snowball, but then gets bigger and bigger, and finally tears everything down with it. It is precisely this fear of such uncontrollable forces that the manipulator uses to their advantage. It starts with a point of view or suggestion, which may sound quite reasonable at first. In the following, he argues, however, that this seemingly harmless suggestion triggers a chain of disastrous consequences that end in a fiasco. This leads him to conclude that the original proposal is unacceptable.

Everyday/practical example:

In a personal interview with your supervisor at work, you ask him for a few days of special leave because you want to move. Your boss is not enthusiastic about this request and replies:

"If every employee comes to me now and asks for special leave, I can close the shop down soon. Imagine what an economic loss it would mean for me if all my employees

suddenly wanted special leave. Just think about it, after all, you are also part of our company. You're a good employee and I can't possibly do without you."

In this example, your supervisor wants to put you on the slide. You turn to him with an individual request, and he projects your wish onto all employees. He completely neglects that it is highly unlikely that ALL his employees will demand special leave because they are moving.

What is your boss trying to do with this manipulation?
On the one hand, he wants to warn you of a certain action (in this case applying for special leave), and at the same time intimidate you. In addition, he combines his manipulation attempt with an emotional component ("You are also part of this company..."). Finally, he tries to emphasize your importance for the company by praising your performance ("You are a good employee and I cannot possibly do without you").

What can you do in this case?
You should first check whether the manipulator, in this case your superior, actually used your expressed wish to derive unpleasant consequences from this. It is often the case that the original conversation positions are somewhat distorted in order to derive particularly dramatic consequences.

Furthermore, the weakness of avalanche arguments lies in the constructed causal chain. An avalanche argument can only be as strong as the causal links it establishes. And here in particular, the manipulator is often involved in causal relationships that are questionable or even untenable.

You can tie in exactly with the causal chain set up for an appropriate reaction to the slide tactics. In many cases, the individual links of this chain are only weakly interlocked. So you can answer with critical questions or the construction of a counter-position. If you want to counter the slide tactics, it is best to pick out the weakest link in the chain.

In a conversation with your boss, for example, you can answer:

"Mr. XYZ, thank you for valuing my work. I like to be part of this company, and I enjoy my work very much. In order to be able to concentrate fully on the well-being of the company, however, I need XY days of special leave, as the move will cost a lot of energy. During this time, I cannot give the company my undivided attention. I also talked to my colleagues and they agreed to represent me in my absence. So you don't have to worry that the team's performance will suffer if I'm away for XY days."

You literally take the wind out of your sails with this answer from your superior. You weaken his dramatic way of argumentation, and go into all links in his chain of argumentation. Now it is up to your superior to find new arguments, which is why he cannot do without you for a few days under any circumstances.

6.2.4 Guarantee tactics

The manipulator vouches for the correctness of his arguments or his point of view with the guarantee tactics. Typical for the use of the guarantee tactic are phrases such as:

- ❖ "You can believe me, that..."

- ❖ "There is no doubt in my mind that..."

- ❖ "I can assure you that..."

- ❖ "I am absolutely convinced that..."

If the manipulator uses such idioms, he gives his word of honour for his point of view, and vouches for the correctness of the statements he makes. But for what reason does he do this?

Guarantee tactics are often used to evade discussion, and at the same time, discharge the burden of proof. In sober terms, there is no reason at all to prove the arguments of the manipulator, because he gives his personal guarantee for the correctness of the assertions he makes. Should the interlocutor still express criticism or doubts after this move, he will possibly give the impression that he wants to question the credibility of the manipulator.

This manipulation technique works particularly well if the manipulator enjoys a good reputation or holds a position of power. Supervisors are very happy to use this tactic with their subordinates.

Everyday/practical example:
You have a visitor from an electrical appliance salesman. In fact, you are interested in a new vacuum cleaner. The salesman praises a certain model of a vacuum cleaner (the most expensive in the range) in the highest tones, including this phrase:

"I can assure you that this vacuum cleaner is the best model on the market. There is absolutely no doubt about it".

Now, you might ask yourself at this point how the agent wants to know whether it is actually the best model on the market - and rightly so, because he owes you proof of this even after you have asked for it. He lacks the arguments to prove his "steep" statement, for example, in the form of test results from renowned institutes. Ultimately, he cannot prove his assertion. Therefore, you have good reason to believe that the seller simply wants to persuade you to make a quick purchase decision, and cannot stand up to a discussion with you as to why this vacuum cleaner model is currently the best appliance on the market.

You can quickly expose warranty tactics by asking your counterpart for evidence for his points of view or statements. If your interviewer is unable to provide such evidence, he or she has most likely used warranty tactics to manipulate you.

6.2.5 Tabooing tactic

This manipulation tactic is often used when an interlocutor wants to avoid and exclude the discussion of certain points of view in advance. These points of view are to a certain extent tabooed.

Why is this tabooing taking place? This can have basically different reasons. It is possible that your interviewer does not want to waste the time with supposedly useless discussions. On the other hand, he may simply want to enforce his position and conceal possible weaknesses of his points of view.

The tabooing tactic is an authoritarian tactic. For this reason, it is particularly effective with people who have a clear position of power. Therefore, superiors in particular like to resort to this manipulation tactic.

Everyday/practical example:
You are in a team meeting with your supervisor. It is an important company decision. A part of the company should be relocated to another location. Your boss enters the room and greets the round with the words:

"Good morning. One thing I would like to make clear right at the beginning. I don't feel like discussing outsourcing to another location. My decision in this matter has already been made."

In this case, your superior will throw all his authority into the balance. If one of the team now stands up against it and opposes it, this could be interpreted as an attempt to shake the balance of power within the company. Your superior wants to take the wind out of your sails from the outset. He already knows how to deal with the outsourcing of the company.

Now how can you resist the tabooing tactics?
An appropriate response to this form of manipulation is particularly difficult and requires a great deal of sensitivity. After all, you must assume that the manipulator uses this tactic for selfish and unnamed motives. If, as in our example, it is also in an appropriate position of power, you risk that this power is directed against you if you veto it. If you are making an already excluded claim, you must be able to justify it very well, for example by pointing out positive effects of your point of view.

In the above example, you will only be able to release your superior from his tabooing tactics if you can give him valid, good arguments to reconsider his decision.

6.2.6 Perfection Trap

The perfection trap is a classic blockade strategy. This tactic is somewhat paradoxical because, it rejects a proposal because it is **not perfect** even though there is **no better solution**. One of the characteristics of the perfection trap is the false conclusion of **unattainable perfection**.

Everyday/practical example:

You would like to visit a musical in Hamburg with your partner. You talk about how you want to travel to Hamburg. You suggest to your partner to fly by plane. He will reply to you:

"Well, I don't really want to fly, because I'm way too insecure about that. Just think of the plane crashes you see on TV all the time."

In this example, the problem of unattainable perfection becomes clear. Your partner is of course right to point out that an aircraft is not an absolutely safe means of transport. However, he will conceal the fact that there may also be train accidents or accidents on the motorway in the car. You can also read about these accidents in newspapers and the news. There is no absolutely safe means of transport that cannot lead to an accident.

In this case, your partner will reject your proposal, even though there is no better solution for safe travel.

This is the case with many situations in life. We hardly ever have an absolutely perfect solution at our disposal. Rather, it is our task to choose from a variety of options, whereby each option can be fraught with risks on its own. So the flaw in thinking about the perfection trap is to criticize a possibility because it is not perfect, even though such perfection cannot be achieved with other solutions.

People who demand perfect solutions misjudge reality. We humans always have only certain options available, which can never be perfect, because not all risks can be excluded. If we could, then we would be gods and almighty.

But why does the manipulator use the perfection trap?
For the manipulator, the perfection trap is practical if he wants to prevent changes or reject suggestions. Basically, he knows (unconsciously) in many cases that there is no perfect solution for a certain proposal or point of view. In this case, he takes advantage of the fact that each option has a weak point somewhere. This makes it almost always possible to block a particular proposal.

As complex as the problem of unattainable perfection may be, the defense against this tactic is comparatively simple and contains two possibilities:

- You directly address the fallacy of unattainable perfection.

- You ask a critical and skilful question.

In our example above, you can inform your partner that statistically speaking, an aircraft is significantly safer as a means of transport than, for example, travelling by train or car.

Alternatively, you can ask him how often he actually hears about crashed airplanes in the news, and whether he knows how many airplanes are on the move around the world every day. In this way, you can make him aware of how small the number of planes is that are actually involved in a dramatic incident.

6.2.7 Irrelevance tactics

When we call something "irrelevant", we want to express that it is unimportant for a certain topic or area of life. If you want to justify a particular point of view or opinion, you have a duty to give real reasons in the reasoning. It is important that the reasons put forward are really relevant to the point of view. If the manipulator provides a reason that has nothing to do with his point of view, then he applies the irrelevance tactic unconsciously or consciously. This tactic is a typical diversionary manoeuvre.

Everyday/practical example:

You want to buy a new smartphone. In an electric shop, you can get advice on which models are currently available on the market. You are interested in a certain device, and have a seller list its advantages for you. Basically, you want to be able to send messages and make phone calls with your smartphone, the rest of the functions don't interest you very much. You then ask the seller if a particular feature is really as important and useful as he claims. He replies somewhat irritated:

"The device has the function XYZ. Are you seriously questioning whether this function makes sense on a smartphone? I can tell you that the manufacturer has spent countless hours developing this smartphone to ensure the best possible customer experience. The result is this smartphone that's way ahead of the competition."

Do you find in this example that the seller really answered your question? Probably not, because he couldn't give you a reason for why and whether the function you questioned really is an added value for you. Instead, he praised the hard work of the developers and the smartphone itself without answering your question. Moreover, the term "best possible customer benefit" is very vague and raises new questions for you (what exactly is this customer benefit?) as well as the statement that this smartphone is far ahead of the competition's products (in what respect?).

The seller doesn't seem to know the answer to your question himself, and instead presents you with some bogus arguments, perhaps in the hope that you will withdraw your question.

The seller's views may be correct, but he forgets that his answers don't match your question. So he's establishing a different position than the one that was being debated.

Irrelevance tactics are often used when the manipulator is exposed to attack, criticism or uncomfortable questions. The crucial thing with this tactic is to give the impression as if one were still on the actual subject. For this reason, the manipulator uses terms that fit the actual subject of discussion as often as possible. In this way, he wants to give the impression that he is actually dealing with the subject of the discussion.

Now, how can you defend yourself against irrelevance tactics?

If you have any doubts as to whether the reasons or answers given by your interviewee are actually relevant, simply ask him or her to explain his or her point of view or opinion again in detail. Should he cite the same dubious reasons again, you can make him aware of the irrelevance of his statements by asking him a critical question. Thus, you give him at the same time, the opportunity to improve his argumentation. If your interviewee has deliberately taken a diversionary action, you should try to clearly lead him back to the actual topic or question.

In the above example, you can draw the seller's attention to the fact that you would like to hear his opinion on whether the XYZ function you are referring to makes sense on a smartphone or whether, as an occasional user, you can do without it. If you want to "open another keg", you can also ask the seller what he understands by the customer benefit he addresses, and why exactly this smartphone is one of the best models on the market.

6.2.8 The trap of principle

Often unconsciously, we humans commit the error of thinking to ignore facts, because they cannot be reconciled with our principles true to the motto "It cannot be what must not be". This is exactly where the principle trap begins. Here, facts are negated or ignored if they stand in the way of firm convictions or principles that we absolutely want to hold on to. This **error of reasoning** is also referred to as the **false conclusion of factual negation**.

We should always test our beliefs and principles against reality - but not vice versa. If facts contradict our beliefs, we must be open to change on this point.

Everyday/practical example:
You talk to an acquaintance and in a conversation, you come across the characteristics that make a good marriage. Your interlocutor is of the firm opinion that every good marriage should often have a fight and really "bang". Otherwise, it is in his opinion not really a good marriage. You spontaneously think of some married couples in your circle of acquaintances of whom you know that they have a very harmonious relationship. You give

this to your interlocutor to consider. However, he replies that such marriages could only be really good superficially, and that this would change with your acquaintances. You would experience that already still.

Obviously, your acquaintance already has turbulent relationships behind him or knows many couples whose quarrels are the order of the day. Of course, it is perfectly normal to quarrel once - this happens in the best marriages and relationships. In our example, however, your acquaintance is firmly convinced that frequent quarrels constitute a good relationship. So, he looks at the world through the glasses of his own principles. You do not share his views and contradict his theory with facts (own experiences). Nevertheless, your interlocutor is not willing to put his theory to the test, but rather reality. In his eyes, this cannot really be as it seems to you. So according to his logic, **YOU** have made a mistake and not **HE**.

Why does your conversation partner fall into the principle trap?
It is often used when a person does not want to look reality in the eye. In some cases, it can also be an expression of pure helplessness, for example to make the world explainable.

The defense of a principle trap can be done in two different ways:

1) You simply ignore the fact that your interlocutor puts his principles above reality.

2) You draw his attention to the fact that he has succumbed to the fallacy of fact negation.

In the above example, you could ask your interlocutor to put his or her general statement about what makes a good marriage or relationship in his or her eyes to the acid test, because you think that a good marriage can do without a lot of quarrelling. You have already experienced this yourself in your circle of acquaintances.

A prerequisite for this, however, is a fundamental willingness on the part of your interviewee to reflect self-critically on your own position or arguments.

6.2.9 Perspective trap

If we prepare decisions, we should know which arguments speak for and which speak against our decision. Then we have to weigh up whether the pro or the contrast side weighs more heavily, and which of the two sides has the better arguments. If one avoids such a pro-and-contra-argumentation, one falls into the trap of the one-sided perspective.

Everyday/practical example:

You are talking to a friend because you are toying with the idea of becoming self-employed. Your friend is very sceptical about this plan. He says to you:

"Well, I wouldn't want to go into business for myself. You have to work all day, have no free time left, and depend on banks to finance your business. Besides, you have a lot less time for your family."

In this case, your friend will focus exclusively on the negative aspects of self-reliance and completely ignore possible advantages. In addition, he obviously tends to exaggerate his arguments. Just because you are self-reliant doesn't mean you have to work all day and give up all your free time with your family.

In this case, your interlocutor avoids **objectively** weighing up the advantages and disadvantages of self-employment. His goal is obviously to get you quickly on his decision side, and to talk you out of your plans for self-employment. Maybe there is concern about your financial situation behind his manipulation attempt. Under certain circumstances, however, he may have had bad experiences with self-employment himself, and is now projecting them onto you. Of course, it does not mean that YOUR jump into self-employment is doomed to failure, just because this may have been the case with your interlocutor.

How can you defend yourself against the perspective trap?

In our example, you should urgently pay attention to whether your interviewer has really examined all perspectives without prejudice in his argumentation, and whether he has dealt with the advantages as well as the disadvantages. Only when he has done this is it possible to make an actual assessment of the situation.

In this case, you can ask the manipulator to also examine the other side, in this case, the advantages of his argumentation. In addition, you can ask critical questions to make your friend understand that he should not look at your plans one-sidedly.

Additional tip:

If we stick to the above example, it will certainly be helpful for you to compile a list of advantages and disadvantages if you have been unsettled by your friend's one-sided argumentation in the conversation. Of course, it should not go unmentioned here that in the end, it is not your interlocutor who has to decide whether you want to start your own business or not, but only yourself.

7. Bonus chapter - Manipulation through nonverbal communication

We humans cannot help but unconsciously or consciously send signals with our bodies. With this body language, our body communicates both with ourselves and with other people. You will hardly believe how often you actually use nonverbal communication in everyday life without even consciously perceiving it, and how you manage to benefit from this knowledge. The better you understand your body signals, the better you will understand your whole being, and the easier it will be for you to communicate successfully with other people.

7.1. What is body language and what function does it fulfil?

Body language is any form of communication that does not use language, but parts of your body. For this reason, body language is also called **nonverbal communication**.

Basically, there are two types of body language:

    (1) Unconscious body signals,

    (2) Conscious body signals

Unconscious body signals

You will surely think it already; the unconscious body signals make up the majority of the human body language.

> Example:
>
> You get a sad or negative message. With your body language, you will react accordingly in the form of a sad or shocked facial expression, sweating hands or a tense posture.

Such unconscious body signals basically fulfil a practical purpose, because they give your environment information about your emotional state. Such body signals are controlled by our body automatically and within fractions of a second. For this reason, it is almost impossible to adapt to such behaviors.

> Example:
>
> If we sympathize with a person or find them attractive, our pupils dilate when we look them straight in the eye.

You can see from this example that you can often not influence unconscious body signals, because whether your pupils dilate or not, you can not consciously control.

Conscious body signals

Conscious body signals are understood to be, for example, a smile during a flirt or a targeted eye contact with the conversation partner.

Example:

The so-called poker face, an absolutely emotionless facial expression to avoid telling the opponent through smiles or other physical reactions.

Body signals that other people use to manipulate their environment. You, too, can influence your counterpart by training certain signals in order, for example, to achieve your conversation goals more easily. These methods are also used by psychologists and psychotherapists to facilitate access to the patient.

7.2. Why is nonverbal communication important?

Every person speaks not only with his mouth, but also with gestures and facial expressions – basically, even with the whole body. This is deeply anchored in a person's subconscious and serves to underline what has been said or to emphasize it.

As the American professor of psychology Albert Mehrabian found out in a study, only seven (!) percent of words in a conversation are responsible for the overall impression we get from a person. According to this study, the tone of voice accounts for 38 percent. The lion's share (55 percent), however, is determined by a person's body language, which impression we have of our counterpart. Amazing: Our body signals therefore have a greater influence on the reaction of our counterpart than the words that we address to our conversation partner.

Surely, you have heard the saying that people communicate with "hands and feet" before. This is no accident, because you can actually communicate with a person whose language is unknown to you. Admittedly, this only works bumpy, and is only suitable for expressing the most elementary things - but it shows how important nonverbal communication is in a person's life.

A person's body language includes the following factors:

- ➢ Gesturing,

- ➢ Facial expression,

- ➢ Pitch,

- ➢ Further physical reactions.

This overall package is ultimately decisive for how our counterpart perceives us, and whether he finds us sympathetic or unappealing, friendly or grumpy, interesting or uninteresting.

Think only of the communication between humans and a dog. A dog can only decipher nonverbal signals of a human being; the verbal language of the human being is unknown to him. For this reason, it doesn't matter what words you say to a dog, the only thing that matters is what your gestures, facial expressions and vocal pitch "speak" to the dog.

7.3 What types of manipulation through nonverbal communication are there?

7.3.1 The power of smiles

It may sound banal, but a smile is one of the most effective ways to positively influence your counterpart. When you smile, you give other people the impression that you are approachable, self-confident and warm-hearted. These things cause other people to trust you quickly.

If we find a person sympathetic, we will sooner or later begin to smile in conversation with him - whether we like it or not. This is a significant form of nonverbal communication, because with a smile, we signal good interests and honest intentions to our conversation partner. We perceive people who smile frequently and gladly as sympathetic and attractive.

What does this mean for you? In order to appear likeable and attractive for your conversation partner, use a smile specifically. This alone can leave a positive impression and create a pleasant atmosphere for the conversation.

The smile is one of the most important means of communication, because it allows us to get in touch with people whose word language we do not understand. A smile is understandable everywhere in the world, and puts us in a positive light. Only by the sympathy which we release with a smile with our interlocutor, we can show completely strange humans that we pursue good intentions.

Small babies at the age of four to eight weeks to use their smile already. A few months later, they even have a feeling for the right timing to influence their fellow human beings with a smile, i.e. manipulate them.

You, too, can use a smile in conversations to achieve your conversation goals more easily, because we are more likely to be influenced or persuaded by people who seem likeable and attractive to us than by people who seem unfriendly or distant to us.

But a smile from you has another quality, because if you smile yourself, it is easier for you to feel sympathy for your counterpart. You suggest to yourself by smiling that you find your interlocutor sympathetic. As a result, you will actually begin to like him.

But there is a small hurdle if you want to become a master of smiling. To be truly authentic, it is important that not only the corners of your mouth but also the corners of your eyes find their way up when you smile.

As French psychologists have found out, a real smile also raises a person's corner of the eye. A fake and artificial smile, on the other hand, does not lift the corner of a person's eye. Therefore, it may take some practice to train your smile to look as natural as possible, so that your "smile tactic" is not exposed by the other person.

In order to start a communication with a smile, you also need some practice, so that a friendly facial expression becomes an automatism for you. Basically, it makes sense to make you aware of your facial expression again and again. If you sit for hours in front of a computer, or if you worry about a problem with your head, this will usually also be reflected in your face. Such a wrinkled face has a negative influence on your mood and well-being.

In fact, Italian researchers have found that we feel more aggressive and angrier when we have been wrinkling our forehead for hours.

So when you realize you've been frowning for hours, take a break. To brighten your facial expression, stand in front of a mirror and correct it. So sometimes, having a smile on your lips is a kind of will decision: You want to be happy and make a conscious decision at that moment.

If you start letting your facial expression appear as if you were happy, you will be happy in the end - as well as the people who come into contact with you.

7.3.2 Mirroring

In psychology, the copying of individual behaviour patterns of the counterpart is called mirroring. For example, if our counterpart drinks a sip of water, we do the same - but not to the same extent or immediately, because this could be interpreted as "mimicry".

Why do we humans do this? By subtly adapting our own body language to that of our counterpart, we unconsciously want to suggest familiarity to our interlocutor. Since we can perceive and find ourselves in the other person by copying different behaviour patterns, our sympathy for the other person increases. It is in the nature of man to feel particularly comfortable among like-minded people. By mirroring the behaviour - i.e. with mirroring - we give our conversation partner the feeling of being such a like-minded person.

By the way, this technique is used professionally by numerous people, for example in areas where increases in turnover are desired. Why? Customers like to spend more money when they are satisfied. Mirroring makes the salesperson appear more likeable to the customer, and the customer unconsciously feels on the same wavelength as the salesperson - partly because the salesperson reflects the customer's behaviour.

How can you use mirroring?

Basically, this method is very easy to use and learn, because you only need a good eye to observe the behaviour of the other person and then apply it yourself in a reasonable dosage.

Example:

In a conversation, take on a pose that is similar to that of your counterpart. But be careful not to take exactly the same pose. For example, if the other person crosses his legs, wait a moment and do the same. Your interviewer crosses his arms in front of his body, waits for a moment and crosses his arms in front of his body. Your interlocutor will unconsciously perceive this mirroring of his behavior, and will have the feeling that you both tick similarly - regardless of what you are talking about.

Pay attention to an open posture

If you tell your conversation partner about one of your ideas, first make sure that you both have an open posture. Arms and legs should not be crossed – otherwise, this is a sign that your counterpart is skeptical. If, on the other hand, he adopts an open posture, you will increase your chances of approval and support considerably.

How can you achieve an open posture in your conversation partner?

You will hardly believe it, but there are actually two proven tricks to move your conversation partner to an open posture, without him noticing anything about it.

Option 1: Lean forward and speak more quietly when you tell your interviewer about your idea. You should not whisper, but speak so softly that the person you are talking to leans forward to you in order to understand you well.

Possibility 2: Give something to your conversation partner, any object, for example a business card or a handout. To accept this object, he must open his posture. This trick is especially useful if your counterpart has taken up an entangled posture so far.

But attention: It is important in any case that you do not give the impression to your conversation partner that you are copying him. Otherwise, he will become skeptical and start to distrust you. Therefore, be careful when you adopt the posture of your counterpart, and refrain from hectic movements. Wait a moment before you adopt the posture of your conversation partner, so that it appears more natural.

7.3.3 Talking with your hands

Studies of human brain waves have shown that the same region of the brain is active when speaking and gesticulating. This means that our language is inextricably linked to our gestures. Therefore, it is understandable why we like to use our hands when talking.

Think here only of a lecture. Imagine a speaker standing stiffly in front of the crowd all the time during his speech. This would certainly be very strange and monotonous. A good lecture lives therefore, not only from an exciting content and good rhetoric, but also from a suitable gesture. In fact, gesticulating in speech also serves a meaningful purpose: it helps us to grasp clear thoughts and formulate understandable sentences. In addition, researchers have found that a speaker is considered more competent by his audience when he gesticulates.

So what does this insight mean to you? Your gestures are very important in communicating with other people, because they help your counterpart to understand you. In addition, you can underline what is said with the appropriate gestures, and achieve your conversation goals more easily with the appropriate gestures. However, you should not exaggerate this body signal: A wild waving of your hands gives the impression of insecurity and nervousness to your listener.

So, don't underestimate the importance of your hands in your next conversations.

7.3.4 Nodding

If you want to get agreement in a conversation and hear a "yes", let your conversation partner nod first before you ask him your actual question.

How can you go about that?

If you have built up sufficient agreement of the body signals with your counterpart and begin to nod, your interlocutor will mirror your body language and also nod. If this is not the case, you start nodding when he talks, as if you agree with his statements. Then nod further when you say something, and you will be able to observe how your counterpart also begins to nod.

Now is the perfect time for your actual question.

Why is nodding so important in this case?

Researchers have found that we are more likely to agree with our counterparts' statements when we nod. Of course, regardless of this, it is helpful if you have good arguments at your disposal to achieve your goal. Just by nodding diligently, you will hardly be able to convince the person you are talking to of your point of view or to get your approval.

7.3.5 Standing Up

As soon as you stand and your conversation partner sits, you have gained the upper hand over the conversation. Why? People who stand seem powerful and dominant to us. The same principle is embodied by bouncers who instil respect in us because they have a powerful and dominant effect on us.

So, you have an advantage when your counterpart sits and you stand. However, it is important to keep the appropriate distance to your interlocutor; otherwise he may quickly feel uncomfortable in your presence. This can unnecessarily aggravate the tense situation, especially during crisis talks or stimulated discussions.

So, if you are in a meeting, use an excuse to get up. This can happen, for example, if you write something on a flipchart or show something on the screen. In this case, it is perfectly legitimate to stand up and none of those present will understand this as a "provocation attempt".

Extra tip: Getting up while talking works particularly well if you are making a phone call to a person. They cannot see what you are doing, but you will find that you feel safe when you get up. The phone conversation will make it easier for you to reach your conversation goals. Why? Your voice will become fuller and clearer as you stand. And during a telephone conversation, the power of your voice is very important - besides your choice of words.

7.3.6 Pay attention to posture

If you are in a conversation with a person, then your body or at least your head will lean towards the person you are talking to. In this way, you show him nonverbally that you are interested in him and what he says. It flatters people immensely if they have the impression that they are interesting for their interlocutor.

You can use this little nonverbal trick to make your counterpart feel important and heard. He will love you for this, and you will get much more approval if you want something from him.

But be careful: Be sure to keep a certain physical distance to your conversation partner. The right measure is crucial in this nonverbal trick. So, you should not get uncomfortably close to your interlocutor and pay attention to his body language. If he moves away from you, you may have exceeded his personal distance limit. No problem; that is not further tragic, if you respect this signal of him and go something on distance. Even with a little more distance, you can turn to him and pay attention to an open posture.

7.3.7 Using your feet

It may sound a bit crazy to you at first, but watch the position of your feet in a conversation! If these point to your conversation partner, this is a positive nonverbal signal. In this way, you show the person that you are interested in him or her and that sympathy exists. Conversely, you can also observe this in your conversation partner.

In fact, our feet are the most honest part of our body in a conversation. Many people pay attention to their gestures and facial expressions, but not to their feet.

You can use this knowledge in a conversation. If you are interested in ending the conversation, simply turn your feet away from your conversation partner. You will see that the conversation is slowly coming to an end. If your feet have turned away from the person you are talking to, the rest of your body will move accordingly. If your whole-body language points towards the door, you subtly make it clear to the person you are talking to that the conversation should end.

If you want to be self-confident in the conversation, widen your stand a little and place your feet shoulder-wide. If you combine this with the upright trick, you will be very self-confident with the person you are talking to, and you will be able to give your statements more meaning. Accordingly, you will be more likely to get approval for your statements and achieve your conversation goals more quickly.

It is actually one of the strongest nonverbal manipulation tactics that only a few people are aware of. You should therefore, remember and train this trick as often as possible in conversations, so that it quickly becomes flesh and blood.

7.3.8 Power Poses

As the American social psychologist Amy Cuddy attests, not only does our hormonal balance lead to dominant behaviour in communication with other people, but it also works the other way round. If a person behaves dominantly, his hormonal balance will also adapt accordingly and become similar to that of successful leaders. **So, if you act dominant, you will also start to think dominant and feel dominant.**

Why is it helpful to feel dominant in conversations with other people? Dominance gives us a sense of power, and power means security. So, if you are dominant in communicating with other people, this will give you a feeling of power and security.

The social psychologist Amy Cuddy distinguishes power posing in two different classes:

(1) High Power Poses

(2) Low Power Poses

High Power Poses

These are behaviors with which you can express dominance, for example:

- crossed arms behind your head,

- a broad sitting posture on a chair or a couch.

High Power Poses are behaviors in which you claim a lot of space (territory) for yourself.

Low Power Poses

Conversely, low power poses are behaviors with which you express nervousness, anxiety, and generally low self-confidence, such as:

- a tight sitting posture,

- angled legs (crouching posture).

How can you use power poses in conversations?

If you are standing in front of an important conversation, for example with a superior, then take High Power Poses first. Make yourself big with these poses. Take a position that outsiders would immediately consider "boss". Through these dominant poses, you will feel strong and secure inwardly - the best prerequisite to appear stable and confident in a conversation with your superior.

7.3.9 Keeping eye contact

Maybe you're more of a shy person, introverted or nervous. Nevertheless, it is important to keep eye contact with the person you are talking to. As a recommended guideline, you should keep eye contact with your interviewer during about half of the conversation.

What happens if you have too little eye contact?
On the one hand, you give the impression to your interlocutor that you are very insecure. For him, this means that you are a potentially easy victim for his manipulation attempts - and that is exactly what you want to prevent.

On the other hand, your interviewer may think you want to hide something from him or even lie to him if you avoid eye contact.

As a rule, we don't really look deep into each other's eyes in conversations. Rather, we have a dreamy look that concentrates more or less on the eye region. If you really want to establish a deep connection with your conversation partner, then really look him in the eye and ask yourself the question, which eye color your conversation partner has. If you can answer this question, you will have good eye contact with him.

7.4. Observing congruence

One speaks of congruence when verbal and nonverbal communication coincide, i.e. when the literal statements are in harmony with the body signals. Accordingly, incongruence means when you act on a statement, but are not absolutely behind it.

Example:

Imagine a person who more or less half-heartedly - without fire and esprit - has to give a lecture or a presentation. The information itself may be very interesting, but the speaker's voice and posture speak a little of a rousing language.

Your first thought was surely that this person does not have to stand in front of you and give a lecture. As a result, you will not be interested in the information presented, and you will look forward to the end of the presentation - just like the speaker himself.

You see that a lack of congruence in conversations can quickly destroy your credibility if your conversation partner perceives this. Therefore, it is important to integrate your body language into your verbal communication. So, smile and keep eye contact during a conversation. Present yourself openly and helpfully. Remember that at the end, 55 percent of the time, it is the congruence that decides whether your counterpart believes your words and is interested in your arguments or not.

7.5. Recognizing and understanding body signals

The human body language is full of signals which, in their entirety, convey a message to their counterparts. When your partner comes home with teary eyes, he doesn't have to explain how he is doing. You can literally read it from his face. The question as to whether he is sad is superfluous, because his body signals have already told you. The only question that will occupy you at this moment is WHY he is sad.

But it is also the small gestures and body signals that play a big role in our communication.

Maybe you are the type of person who likes to cross his arms in front of his chest in a conversation. You are not alone in this, because many people perceive this as a comfortable pose. However, you can unintentionally leave another person with a defensive or disinterested impression, even if this is not your intention.

If you play with your shirt collar in a conversation or scratch your face again and again, this can be interpreted by a person with communication experience as a signal of nervousness. He may then try to test you and manipulate you for his arguments.

On the other hand, you can, of course, also interpret appropriate signals and infer from them how your conversation partner feels. This can help you decide how you should behave in the conversation, depending on your intentions and goals. This will help you to assess your chances in critical conversations, and to manipulate your interlocutors in your favour.

If, for example, your conversation partner takes a low power pose (e.g. a closed and tight sitting posture), you will most likely be able to take over the dominant part in the conversation. If the pupils of the other person contract during the conversation (pay attention to eye contact), this is often a sign of stress. Your interviewer is therefore, under pressure, which makes him more receptive to manipulation.

People who generally tend to take passive poses in conversations are very likely to be inclined to give in and accept unfavourable conditions for them, even in conflicts.

The correct interpretation and understanding of body language is therefore a powerful instrument at your disposal.

7.6 Body language: Practice makes perfect

Reading another person's body language is a complex task. Nonverbal behavior itself is a difficult matter, since every person is different, and can also present his or her body language in a different way. If you want to read another person's body language, it is important to look at the whole picture.

So this means that if you want to understand another person's body signals, you need to consider several factors, such as:

- ✓ their personality,
- ✓ social factor
- ✓ the surroundings,
- ✓ etc.

Every person has a complex personality - so it is not surprising that a person's body language is also a complex matter.

> Example:
> You can compare reading and interpreting body language to watching your favorite TV show. Would it be possible for you to pick out just one scene and deduce the content of the entire episode from it? Surely this is not feasible. You need more information about the actors and their personalities, some of which have been highlighted in past episodes. It is therefore important that you can view the

entire picture - the same applies to reading and correctly interpreting a person's body language.

Don't forget that every person is different. Therefore, it is very difficult to establish universal rules for the correct interpretation of a person's body language. The longer you have been able to study this person and their body language, the better you will succeed, because what may be valid for one person may not be valid for another.

Example:
Some people can't look you in the eye when they confront you with lies. Others, on the other hand, try to keep eye contact spasmodically, so that they are not suspected of lying to you.

So you shouldn't judge a person hastily solely on the basis of his body language. Nonverbal signals are only one factor that can give you information about a person's condition.

Think of visiting a doctor. You turn to the doctor because you have pain in your knee. The doctor will first examine you, and then make a **suspicion-diagnosis**. However, this can only be really confirmed with the help of further examinations, such as X-rays or MRI.

The same applies to reading a person's body language. This will give you initial indications of what is going on in the person, but you will only get a reliable "diagnosis" if you get to know this person better and/or if your counterpart provides you with further body signals.

7.7. Practical exercises for applying nonverbal manipulation techniques

In order to learn and practice the nonverbal manipulation techniques mentioned above, it is important to apply them as often as possible in practice, i.e. in everyday situations. You will find simple exercises for many of these techniques, which you can easily implement yourself.

Mirroring

Observe the behaviour and posture of your conversation partner, and try to copy individual body signals, such as the sitting position, the posture of the hands or smaller activities, such as occasional drinking from a glass.

Smiling

Give your conversation partner a friendly facial expression. Smile at him and make sure that the corners of your eyes also find their way up. Remember that a smile has a positive effect on your mood - not only on that of your conversation partner, but also on your own.

Power Poses

Take high power poses whenever the time and opportunity present themselves. Through this alpha behavior you will become more confident in all the things you do. Watch your counterpart's pose in the conversation. Is he more of a low power pose or a high-power pose? Based on his pose, you can conclude how your interlocutor sees himself in the hierarchy between the two of you.

Congruence

In conversations, make sure that your body language also reflects what you would like to communicate to your conversation partner. If you try to convince him of your points of view and arguments, he should clearly feel your passion and openness for this topic. So send him body signals that seem interested. Then, your counterpart will react accordingly with interest, and it will be easier for you to reach your conversation goals.

Using and understanding signals

During the conversation, pay attention to the facial expressions and gestures of your conversation partner. The hands and eyes in particular often reveal a lot about a person's emotional state. For example, pay attention to whether your interlocutor is in an open or crossed pose, and how often he seeks and maintains eye contact with you. Also, the size of the pupils as well as their change during the conversation can be a good indicator for the actual emotional state of the person you are talking to.

7.8. Concluding words on nonverbal manipulation

In this bonus chapter, you have received a lot of information about nonverbal signals and their effects in conversations. If you save this information and consider it in future conversations, you will be able to assess the condition of your counterpart much more easily, and it will be easier for you to deal with your interlocutor.

This knowledge can be very useful in various situations. It will be easier for you to understand your fellow human beings both in your private and professional life. If you not, only perceive their words, but also hidden body signals. It will be easier for you to make a good impression with your superiors and business partners, to build and maintain good relationships with customers and to make new friendships - in short, it will be easier for you to achieve your conversation goals.

During your first "training lessons", first pay attention to your own behavior, and try to perceive yourself in conversations with other people. How do you react when you are nervous or excited? What body signals do you send out when you are unsure? Through this information, you will gradually become more sensitive to the subject of body language, and it will become easier and easier for you in the future to recognize and correctly assess the body signals of other people.

8. Conclusion

Every human being strives from birth to have his needs and desires fulfilled. This is done through communication with other people. For this reason, attempts to manipulate conversations often take place unconsciously. Also, you yourself manipulate the people in your environment (consciously or unconsciously) in order to reach your personal goals and to get your needs satisfied. In this book, you have certainly seen this with many examples.

If you know and understand the different forms of manipulation attempts, you can successfully defend yourself against them - with other people as well as with yourself. This happens with the help of defense tactics, which you got to know in this book. Of course, it is important that you use these defense techniques regularly and consciously, so that they become flesh and blood and eventually become automatisms. If you have succeeded in this, you are well prepared against the various attempts at manipulation, which are poured into you day after day in conversations or in the media. Don't forget at this point that practice makes perfect, and that no master has yet fallen from heaven.

I hope that with this book, I could sensitize you to the topic of manipulation attempts and awaken your curiosity. Of course, this guide cannot claim to be complete. This means that there are countless attempts at manipulation, of which I have, however, presented the most important ones to you in this reading.

I wish you now much success with attentive listening in discussions with your fellow men. Surely, you can unmask manipulation attempts already in first conversations with other humans and react with the help of the presented defense techniques adequately to it.

I would be pleased if you would understand this book as a suggestion to familiarize yourself even more with the topic of manipulation tactics at some point. I can guarantee that this will be an exciting project for you.

Your Alexander Hellmoldt

Legal notice and imprint

This work, including all contents, is protected by copyright. Reprinting or reproduction, in whole or in part, as well as storage, processing, reproduction and distribution with the aid of electronic systems, in whole or in part, is prohibited without the written permission of the author. All translation rights reserved.

The contents of this book have been researched from recognized sources and checked with great care. Nevertheless, the author does not assume any liability for the topicality, correctness and completeness of the information provided.

Liability claims against the author, which refer to damages of health or material kind, which were caused by use or misuse of the presented information and/or by the use of incorrect and incomplete information, are in principle impossible if on the part of the author, as can be proven, deliberate or accidental negligence are not present. This book is no substitute for medical or professional advice and care.

Copyright Alexander Hellmoldt
Edition 06/2019
No Section of the text may be used in any form without the consent of the Author.
Contact: Tim Ong/Türkstr. 4/30167 Hannover
Cover photo: Anton Khrupin /shutterstock.com
Formatting: Alexander Hellmoldt

www.ingramcontent.com/pod-product-compliance
Lightning Source LLC
LaVergne TN
LVHW041322200726

843509LV00009B/575